William L. Flowers

CREATION – EVOLUTION and a NATION in DISTRESS

William E. Nowers Capt. USN (ret)

Copyright © 2008 by William E. Nowers

All rights reserved. No part of this book shall be reproduced or transmitted in any form or by any means, electronic, mechanical, magnetic, photographic including photocopying, recording or by any information storage and retrieval system, without prior written permission of the publisher. No patent liability is assumed with respect to the use of the information contained herein. Although every precaution has been taken in the preparation of this book, the publisher and author assume no responsibility for errors or omissions. Neither is any liability assumed for damages resulting from the use of the information contained herein.

ISBN 0-7414-4718-5

Published by:

INFINITY
PUBLISHING.COM

1094 New DeHaven Street, Suite 100
West Conshohocken, PA 19428-2713
Info@buybooksontheweb.com
www.buybooksontheweb.com
Toll-free (877) BUY BOOK
Local Phone (610) 941-9999
Fax (610) 941-9959

Printed in the United States of America

Printed on Recycled Paper

Published April 2008

CREATION – EVOLUTION and a NATION in DISTRESS

	Page
Acknowledgments	iii
Foreword	v
Chapter One: Definitions and Explanations	1
Chapter Two: Intelligent Design and Irreducible Complexity	9
Chapter Three: Beginning of Life	19
Chapter Four: Microevolution & Macrovolution	31
Chapter Five: Missing Links	38
Chapter Six: Conspiracy of the Scientists	45
Chapter Seven: A Godly Nation, Adrift	58
Chapter Eight: Theistic Evolution	76
Chapter Nine: Legislation and The Courts	92
Chapter Ten: What Can We Do?	102
Bibliography	108
Figure 1. Life Begins	22
Figure 2. Siamese Bull Cat	39
Figure 3. A Fishy Story	40
Figure 4. Reptile Flight School	42

ACKNOWLEDGMENTS

I want to thank my wife, Millie for her careful and detailed review of the many different roughs I had to write. I am a terrible writer and must write and rewrite several times to achieve what I hope is a clear and convincing argument for creation and for good old American patriotism.

I also want to thank Matthew Chandler for his valuable comments and for drawing the figures, Pastor Mark Dunn for his review and comments, Larry Ingels for his review and Cindy Brown for her review and gracious unsolicited (really) comments. There are others who assisted in reviewing the manuscript, _____ and _____ (you know who you are)

The politically correct thing is to absolve those who assisted in this effort and claim that any mistake is mine alone. As you will discover as you read this, I am not politically correct. With the exception of my wife, who is always right, I sought the assistance of others so if any errors are found, you can blame them.

Lest anyone think I am a complete boob, I am on occasion even politically correct. For example, I can clearly state, that no animals were harmed in the writing of the manuscript or the publishing of this book.

CREATION-EVOLUTION and a NATION in DISTRESS

FOREWORD

In recent years dozens of new books, videos and DVD's have become available on both creation and evolution. Also books, articles and movies that portray Christians as losers, dummies, or just plain ignorant, are in the hundreds. Christian morality is ridiculed while all sorts of immoral acts are glorified. This book presents no new scientific discoveries. It is different in that it attempts to clearly identify the underlying problems facing our society and to offer some practical suggestions in the final chapter.

There are two mutually exclusive world views of the origins of our universe and mankind, creation or evolution. One is a God centered creation as clearly described in Genesis while the other is an atheistic view point that believes everything originated by natural means. "Natural" means no miracles, no input by God and in fact, no God. The late Dr. D. James Kennedy, Pastor of Coral Ridge Ministries and founder of "Evangelism Explosion," put it well when he stated, "We live in a time when there are only two religions competing for the minds, hearts, and loyalties of Western man. One of those religions is Christianity; the other religion is evolution."

Many Americans have been totally convinced that Darwinian evolution has been proven and is, therefore, an accepted fact. Evolution is the politically accepted belief in all our public school biology books, and schools from kindergarten to college. But Darwinian evolution, the amoeba to man concept, is not a scientific fact. It is not even a scientific theory, it is merely an hypothesis. That is scientific talk for guess. Every scientific study and discovery by Darwin proved only microevolution. Everything written by Darwin and all other evolutionists that claim to prove evolution, really involve microevolution only. Darwin provided a great service in showing how a species contains many variations and how survival of the fittest resulted in minor changes within a species. His Galapagos finches are a typical example. But Darwin erred in assuming, with no scientific examples, or evidence, that these minor variations could lead to a new species. This is discussed in more detail in Chapter 4. Darwinian evolution will probably someday appear in the Guinness book of records as the biggest scientific error ever presented to mankind, even exceeding the original belief that the earth was flat.

There is no attempt to portray both sides of this issue as equally honorable, or in reality, just searching for the truth. On the contrary, hard core evolutionists that really dominate the so called politically correct evolution belief, reveal neither honor nor integrity.

This book is admittedly a hard core support for Christianity, the Bible as God's written word and the clear foundation of America as a Christian nation. This book is a direct challenge to our increasingly anti-Christian government agencies, courts, schools and yes, even some of our churches. In Chapter 9, our judicial system is exposed as part of the atheistic, anti-Christian efforts.

Many controversial issues are discussed in considerable detail. A clear and convincing denial of Darwinian evolution is presented as well as a strong support for the creation belief. The impact of undermining the very foundations of this nation, being based on Christian principles, is also an important part of this book.

Evolutionists and anti-Christians intentionally use incomplete quotes, half truths, irrelevant logic, false science and misleading statements in attempting to prove their erroneous beliefs. The deceit, lies and misrepresentations are so persuasive, and have been accepted by our society for so long, it will be difficult for some to believe what is obvious. The fact is that our primary scientific agency in the nation, the National Academy of Sciences, has degenerated to become an atheist dominated agency that will accept no evidence if it supports a Christian belief in creation or a young earth, or if it even questions Darwinian evolution. The organization has even gone so far as to redefine science in order to eliminate any evidence that might support the creation views. No scientific papers can be published concerning creation or evolution without first being peer reviewed. Peer review means getting approval by dogmatic Darwinian evolutionists. More information on the National Academy of Sciences is covered in considerable detail in Chapter 6.

Footnotes are not used to present a more informal and direct presentation of the information. Any direct quotes are referenced in the text. Other reference material used, but not directly quoted, is listed in the bibliography. A very important part of the entire discussion is a clear definition of the words we use. Many previously published books and articles do not define or explain their terms, in some cases, intentionally, hoping to deceive or mislead the reader. At the very beginning, an entire chapter is devoted to definitions and explanations so there will be no doubt what is meant by the words evolution, microevolution, macroevolution and others

Before reading all the material and evidence in this book, one thing should be kept in mind. It is a fact that macroevolution, or a random change to a new and improved species, is impossible. The unbelievably microscopic complexity of living cells, that exist in their own little microscopic world, have no concept that they are part of an eye, or a foot, or whatever, and could not possibly have started by chance. It is a fact that matter cannot create intelligence. To think that these millions of microscopic living cells, all programmed to do what ever they do, can change from being part of an arm, to a wing with feathers, is nothing but pure fantasy. Darwin's belief in evolution was 100% true for microevolution and 100% false for macroevolution. We will never be able to prove what happened 5,000, 10,000, or a million years ago. We can only provide evidence today that might tend to support or deny whatever beliefs we have.

The importance of the evolution belief in the history of this nation is also discussed. While most Americans are well aware of the widespread and increasing immorality that has become endemic in the last 50 years, very few have even attempted to ascribe a common cause to this trend. The real connection of atheistic Darwinian evolution as the underlying cause of the degradation of morality in America, and our retreat from Christianity, is discussed in Chapter 7.

The final chapter proposes some specific actions where every concerned citizen can get involved, to challenge the evolution fraud, and return this nation to its Christian foundation.

This book consists of only 111 pages. A subject of this importance could easily contain a thousand pages or more, and referenced dozens of other books. I could have listed all the so called missing links and skulls promoted by evolutionists. I could have listed hundreds of examples proving our Christian heritage. I could have mentioned and refuted hundreds of claims made by evolutionists. I could have written a chapter on the Scopes monkey trial in 1925, and how the modern version, made into the movie "Inherit the Wind", is still being shown in our public schools as a completely false, and biased, anti-Christian propaganda film.

I could have mentioned many legal cases by our Supreme Court, and lower courts, that deny our Christian heritage, deny fair jury trials for Christians, and in fact, promote atheism or some fringe religion. I could have pointed out dozens of specific errors in our public school biology books, but this is covered in detail in an entire book "Evolution Exposed" by Roger Patterson.

For those who are honestly interested in seeking truth and saving this great nation under God, there is enough information in this book to be convincing. Others, who already have their mind made up, will not be convinced no matter what is written.

CHAPTER ONE

DEFINITIONS AND EXPLANATIONS

Why a separate chapter on definitions? Because the most important part of any controversy is a clear definition and complete understanding of the words we use. In many of our books and articles concerning creation, evolution and Christianity, a clear understanding is completely missing.

Words have definite and fixed meanings. It is amazing to me that most books on this subject do not bother to clearly define exactly what they are discussing. One of many examples is a book by The National Academy of Sciences, on teaching evolution, that doesn't even mention the words microevolution or macroevolution. (details are in chapter 6) When I questioned as to why these words were not even mentioned, the response was, they chose not to. I don't blame them. If I were trying to defend an impossible position, I would certainly not bring up something that would destroy my arguments. Any controversy should start with a clear understanding and definition of the terms and words used.

In any controversy or debate, there are many tactics available to use in order to cloud the opponent's viewpoints, or confuse the evidence. If the reader is forewarned of the many misleading techniques, frequently used by evolutionists, he will be better able to see through the false arguments and misleading words when they are presented.

There was this story of a man looking for odd jobs. He knocked on the front door of a prosperous looking house and when a lady came to the door he said he was looking for work and did the lady have any odd jobs for him to do. She thought for a minute and then said, "Yes, there is some green paint and a brush in the back and I would like you to paint the porch". The worker agreed and proceeded to the back yard. About two hours later he came back to the front door, rang the bell and when the lady arrived he told her he was finished. She paid him and as he was walking away he turned and said, "Oh, by the way, that's not a Porsche, it's a Ferrari."

Another incident involved a farmer who told his hired worker, "we have been having trouble with that horse, he might be getting lame. I would like the horse shod." A few hours later the farmer asked the hired hand where he had been. "All I asked you to do was shod the horse." "Shod the horse", the worker replied, "I thought you said you wanted the horse shot. I've been burying that horse."

Simple understandings, sometimes humorous, but can sometimes have disastrous results. The creation-evolution controversy is loaded with misunderstandings and in many cases they are intentional, in order to support an otherwise unsupportable belief.

Creation: The Christian belief that God created everything in six days, as clearly stated in Genesis. It refers to the start of all life and cannot be compared with evolution which refers, not to the start of life, but to how life may have progressed after it started. The evolutionist's counter to creation, would be their rather nebulous suggestion that life maybe started in some pre-historic pond, by some inert matter, coming together in some unknown fashion, and viola! Matter created intelligence. A spark of life resulted in a living cell, or something equivalent to that. What is even more ridiculous is the reactions of Dr. Frances Crick, co-discoverer of the DNA molecule. He realized that the unbelievably complex structure of the DNA molecule, couldn't have just developed by itself. Being an avowed atheist he could not even consider creation by God, so he claimed life must have come from some other planet. He called it Panspermia.

Atheist: One who believes there is no God. The term itself is not derogatory, but merely describes a person by his belief.

Big Bang: Evolutionists believe that all matter in the Universe was, at one time, in a single point of zero dimensions. Approximately 15 billion years ago it exploded at a fantastically high temperature. Expanding matter later collected into the stars and planets we have today.

Evolution: Is a generic term, used by many different groups, and simply means a change over time. Everyone agrees that nearly everything changes over time. It is ridiculous to argue about evolution without further defining exactly what you are referring to.

Microevolution: For living creatures, evolution must be further defined in order to make any sense. Micro evolution refers to minor changes within a species. This word is seldom used in other books of this same subject, probably because they wanted to stay away from big words. But if it is broken down to micro meaning small, and evolution, meaning change, it becomes easy to understand. It is simply a small change. All new life is the result of the combination of genetic material from each parent. The wide variety of genetic information available in each species allows, for example, all the different skin colors in the human race. Many animals and birds can be bred to emphasize or de-emphasize certain characteristics. Or certain characteristics can be altered in nature by natural means, that is, by natural selection. A main point here is that microevolution involves no new information, but only various and differing combinations of existing genetic information.

Macroevolution: For living creatures it refers to a change from one species to a more advanced species through the introduction of new genetic information, not present in either parent. The new information would be created by a mutation or error in reproduction that resulted in a more advanced or favorable species and this favorable error could be inherited by offspring. This mutation, followed by a succession of beneficial mutations, could result in a new species. Again, this big word is generally omitted in other books concerning this subject. But if broken down to its true meaning, macro means big and evolution means a change. It merely refers to a big change. Macroevolution is the key to the entire Darwinian evolution, amoeba to man, concept.

Darwinian evolution: Evolution of all life forms from initially inert matter, through a series of favorable, but undirected, species changes caused by natural selection, involving macroevolution, leading to all the living species we have today. It is also referred to as amoeba to man evolution.

Theistic evolution: A belief by some Christians that believe science has proven some parts of the Bible, especially the Genesis account of creation, cannot possibly be true. They wish to retain their belief in the Christian God so they are willing to re-interpret various parts of the Bible in an attempt to compromise what they believe science has proven concerning God's word in the Bible. Theistic evolution takes several forms and is discussed more in Chapter 8.

Species: Probably what the Bible in Genesis refers to as Kinds. One biology book, "Biological Science, A Molecular Approach" BSCS Blue Version, Seventh edition, defines species as "…in general, a group of closely related organisms capable of breeding, or mating, to produce fertile offspring with each other, but not with members of other groups." All species were created by God during the original six day creation. Any new species that might be created by macroevolution would seem to be in conflict with Genesis. Evolutionists, at times, refer to a sub-species resulting from speciation as a new species. But this separation of a group for a time, and then failing to interbreed after reuniting, is the result of a loss of genetic information, and could never lead to a new and advanced species.

Speciation: Defined by the evolutionists as creating a new species. But the process involves the splitting of a species into two groups, through the loss of genetic information. It is discussed in more detail in Chapter 4.

Singularity: A term used by evolutionists to explain the unexplainable, and never repeated, Big Bang.

Logic: One definition is "the science of reasoning." Reason is defined as "...intellectual faculty by which conclusions are drawn from premises." We could also include the term "common sense" here, but in today's society, what was once considered common sense, has been overshadowed by what is referred to as "politically correct."

An example of logic and common sense would be, is an obviously true statement, always true? For example if one would ask the question is two plus two four? The obvious answer is yes. But if I ask, "Is two plus two always four?" That makes a difference. Two pounds of sand with two pounds of water will equal four pounds of mixture. But two gallons of sand and two gallons of water will not equal four gallons of mixture. Evolutionists frequently use a false logic similar to the above example in order to mislead and gain support for their false beliefs.

Conflict: In any debate or presentation of conflicting views, there are many tactics that might be used in order to falsely convince others of an erroneous position. Evolutionists, who for the most part have an agenda and are not inhibited by any moral restraints, use many such methods. One example is to attempt to discredit scientific evidence supporting creation solely because it supports the Christian religion. Another is to present evidence to support evolution, when the same evidence also could support creation. Stephen J. Gould once said, "We know evolution is true, because we are here." It makes no more sense in proving evolution than if I said, "We know creation is true because we are here." Another example used to mislead, is to present something that is completely true, without question, and then imply it supports evolution when in fact it had no relation to evolution. Or in a contrarian manner, present something undesirable and falsely attempt to associate it with creation.

The misuse, of the word evolution, by evolutionists, is probably their most flagrant abuse of logic. Proof of microevolution is frequently presented and then is used as evidence for macroevolution. Of course the evolutionists merely use the word evolution all the time, so they can slide back and forth from one to the other, without the uninformed being aware of the so called bait and switch. It is intentionally misleading to say the least. A publication of the National Academy of Sciences, in 1998, titled "Teaching About Evolution and the Nature of Science," uses the word evolution at least dozens, if not hundreds of times. (I didn't count them) It was pointed towards teaching about evolution in the public schools. In the entire 140 pages you will not find the words microevolution or macroevolution used even once, obviously meant to be misleading.

A Christian Nation: In referring to the United States, the foundation of all our laws, our public institutions and our public moral values are all based on the religion of Christianity.

Satire: To ridicule, irony, to express folly, greatly exaggerate. Example: Rush Limbaugh claims he is on loan from God, and argues with half his brain tied behind his back, just to make it fair. If you don't recognize this as satire, you may have trouble with parts of this book.

Miracle: An event or occurrence caused by God that defies any scientific explanation.

Irreducible Complexity : A system made up of many parts working in series, is irreducible if the failure of any one part would cause failure of the system. Considered a proof of intelligent design.

Intelligent Design: A system that shows it did not or could not create itself without any intelligence involved. I.D. is used to explain why complex systems need a designer. Evolutionists deny any attempt to prove there is intelligent design in any species. They know, as does anyone with the intelligence above that of first grader, that the Intelligent Designer would necessarily be God.

Misunderstandings: Whether accidental or intentional can lead to disaster. Raymond B. Lech in his book, "All The Drowned Sailors," reported the following. Near the end of World War II, due to the intensified communications in the Western Pacific, a letter was signed by Vice Admiral Charles

McMorris, Nimitz's Chief of Staff, to all western Pacific Commands, containing the words, "Arrival reports shall not be made for combatant ships." The assumption from this order was that if the arrival of a warship was not to be reported, neither was the non arrival.

On July 30, 1945, the heavy cruiser "USS Indianapolis," while en route to Leyte in the Philippines, was torpedoed and sunk within minutes, and without an SOS being heard by anyone. The failure to report the non arrival of the ship, along with several other minor misunderstandings, resulted in the survivors spending three days in the ocean, before being discovered. Had the ships non arrival on schedule at Leyte been reported, or several other minor misunderstandings not occurred, it is probable that hundreds more could have been saved, and greatly reduced the final cost of 880 lives. It was the U.S. Navy's greatest Sea disaster. Misunderstandings, and a failure to clearly communicate, is also a key problem in the creation-evolution controversy.

Pro-Life: The term pro-life has different meanings to different people. The proper meaning of the term, as it was first coined and became popular, is better defined as anti-abortion. It referred only to the lives being destroyed in the mother's womb. But not wanting to sound negative, the anti-abortion forces adopted the pro-life label. This soon led to unintended consequences when it was picked up and used by the forces that were opposed to capital punishment. You might think that the difference between killing an unborn baby and executing a convicted murderer, or mass murderer, would be obvious to everyone. Oh how naïve you are. Those opposed to all capital punishment have infiltrated and taken over the pro life movement. Some anti abortion groups have succumbed to the forces opposing capital punishment and consider it as part of the pro life movement. Even the Catholic Church, long an opponent of abortion, and for centuries a supporter of capital punishment, is now strongly opposed to the execution of nearly all murderers.

Assumptions: Taken to be true - accepted. An erroneous assumption can result in everything based on that assumption to be false. Evolutionists assume life started in some manner in a prehistoric pond or ocean depths, where matter formed a single living cell. Matter creating intelligence defies any scientific logic. Life starting from non life defies the scientific definition of biogenesis. The very basis of macroevolution is scientifically false.

Impossible: Not possible or not capable of happening. Evolutionists believe the impossible can happen if given millions of years, or a very long time.

Uniformitarianism: The physical processes operating in the material universe, remain the same from the earliest appearance up to the present, or the present is the key to the past. Now this is a big word for most Americans. But size is relative. Consider a really big word like the little fish in the Hawaiian song, "Where the humahumanukanukaapawaa goes swimming by." That is a big word. The other one doesn't seem so big now, does it?

Politically correct: A term that has become popular in recent years that has, essentially replaced freedom of speech. Our society, led by the news media, has determined that certain forms of speech are no longer permitted. This is especially true, but not limited, to the creation controversy. No public school teacher can criticize evolution without fear of his job being in jeopardy. We have not yet made politically correct departures a criminal offense, such as in Canada and Germany where even mentioning that the holocaust didn't happen will get you jail time. But it is coming. Existing and proposed hate crime laws can be interpreted to include speech.

CHAPTER TWO

INTELLIGENT DESIGN and
IRREDUCIBLE COMPLEXITY

Intelligent design and Irreducible complexity are two sides of the same coin. When evaluated, they completely refute the Darwinian evolution belief that life forms can increase in complexity, merely by chance, with no intelligence, or direction involved. Anyone with half a brain can look around him and see many things that could not be built or created without some intelligence behind it. If one looks far enough he will probably see people. If you are reading this, you are one. Probably the most complex thing on this earth is the human brain. To think any part of a complex human body could happen and exist all by itself, with no intelligent input, has to require a faith far greater than that required of Christians. The Darwinian belief that everything started by chance and everything then evolved upward, accidentally, and completely undirected, to all our present life forms, is incredulous. Future generations will probably look back at our present society in amazement wondering how we could have been so stupid.

If the complexity of the human brain does not impress you, how about considering a human being at the very start of a new life? At conception, a human is even smaller than the period at the end of this sentence. It has all the information in it to completely define a human body with all its parts, in the minutest detail, including the blood circulation system, hair, fingerprints, eyes, etc. It would take an entire library to even list the systems that are completely defined, within that small human starting cell. Can you even conceive, of trying to define, to a computer, everything necessary to identify a human body? Yet evolutionists claim all this happened by chance.

Darwin once said that if it could be shown that any physical feature could not be formed gradually, by natural selection, then his theory would fail. Can we come up with a single feature that can not be formed gradually? This is almost a joke. By today's scientific standards and knowledge, Darwin's statement seems unbelievably antiquated since the latest scientific evidence at the microscopic level, proves that physical features can neither be formed nor improved, by natural selection.

Darwin's basic belief that all life evolved from lesser life forms may have had some semblance of reality in the scientific world of 150 years ago. The electron microscope had not been invented, microscopic details of cellular structure in living species was unknown and by today's standards, medical studies were still rather primitive. All of Darwin's scientific evidence that attempted to support his beliefs, supported microevolution only. He had not a single example of one species ever changing to a more advanced species. All of Darwin's writings merely assumed that examples of microevolution automatically gave credibility to macroevolution, without a shred of evidence. Without evidence then, why is this even an issue today? Because the atheist dominated evolutionists will never admit defeat. Evidence and truth mean nothing to them if it denies, or even questions their dogmatic belief in a new Darwinian god, or if it supports intelligent design.

There is a sharp distinction between animals and humans. Darwin denied this and attempted to show, but only through his own deductions and beliefs, that animals evolved into humans. No evidence by Darwin, nor any scientist since has shown proof that any animal ever evolved into a human. A later chapter discusses the definition of life. My definition also includes the requirement, that the spark of life, is God given.

There is also a sharp distinction between microevolution and macroevolution. Darwin merely assumed that his observed variations within a species would, over millions of years, account for changes to a new species. No real evidence or example was ever provided by Darwin and no proof exists today of any accidental change to a new and improved species.

An entire book could be written on the microscopic complexities of living cells and the impossibility of these cells creating themselves bit by bit over millions of years. And, in fact, such a book was written. Michael Behe is a research scientist and Associate Professor of Biochemistry at Lehigh University. Mr. Behe's book, titled "Darwin's Black Box", really puts the final nail in the coffin of Darwinian evolution. Mr. Behe gives several examples of irreducible complexity including a mouse trap, a Rube Goldberg device, blood clotting, and others,

Probably the most impressive example is his discussion of a cell's cilium. The cilium is the fine hair like tail in some cells that moves back and forth to propel the cell though its liquid medium. This cilium is so fine it shows up on the most powerful light microscope, only as a fine hair. But under an electron microscope, a cross section of the cilium reveals an internal tubular structure that contains nine pairs of microtubes surrounding two central microtubes, each joined by spokes and links. Mr. Behe shows this 9+2 structure is irreducibly complex in that the failure of any of the microscopic components would result in the system's failure. It is hard for us to even imagine the microscopic size and complexity of this tubular structure, all being within a fine hair so small it hardly shows up on a normal light microscope. One might think that would settle the discussion and, as Dr. Duane Gish, the well known and very successful creation debater from the Institute for Creation Research, would say, "Well that settles it, we may as well all go home."

But atheists have an agenda which is to never accept solid scientific evidence if it supports creation or discredits Darwinian evolution. Several scientists have challenged Behe's arguments, not about the irreducible complexity, but about his claim the system could not possibly occur randomly, by chance. Given enough time and a wild enough imagination, anything is possible, according to the evolutionists. This reminds me of the lady who told a suitor that she would marry him, only if he were the last man on earth. He replied "then there's a chance." This is the kind of chance evolutionists have.

While Mr. Behe is a supporter of irreducible complexity, he is not a creationist. He is not trying to bring religion into the issue and he has not seen fit to accept the God of the Bible. He is just a scientist presenting scientific research. He does not even suggest that the intelligent designer is God. However it is obvious to anyone, and especially to the evolutionists, that the only possible designer is God. Of course this is why they are so adamant in denying the obvious. The sub title to Mr. Behe's book is "The Biochemical challenge to Evolution". Mr. Behe does not even identify the difference between micro and macroevolution. In his first Chapter, he implies that he basically supports Darwin's evolution, while mentioning only examples of microevolution.

One of the many stubborn theistic evolutionists is Kenneth R. Miller and in his book "Finding Darwin's God" with a sub title of "A Scientist's search for common ground between God and evolution," he tries to discredit Behe's proof of irreducible complexity. Mr. Miller, first of all is one of the evolutionists that believe they can solve the entire issue by simply compromising. Of course their idea of a compromise is to accept anything that doesn't challenge Darwinian evolution.

Mr. Miller's challenge to irreducible complexity is to claim complex systems can gradually occur merely by natural selection. Concerning blood clotting, he stated:

> "The key to understanding the evolution of blood clotting is to appreciate that the current system did not evolve all at once…The powerful opportunistic pressures of natural selection progressively recruited one gene duplication after another, gradually fashioning a system in which high efficiencies of

controlled blood clotting, made the modern vertebrate circulatory system possible."

To be honest, this is all a bunch of baloney. Talking about "powerful opportunistic pressures...progressively recruiting gene duplication" etc... is nothing more than words, with no proof, or evidence of any of this. In referring to species with arms, that evolved into wings, Mr. Miller stated:

"Its easy to show living examples of forelimbs only partly modified for flight that have useful functions as gliding appendages. Half a wing, under the right circumstances, can be very useful."

This is another ridiculous comment with no supporting evidence, because there isn't any. While these comments are lifted out of the entire book, they are not taken out of context since anti-creation, Darwinian evolution, is the context of the book.

As a side issue Stephen Jay Gould wrote an entire book on the subject of compromise. It was titled, "Rocks of Ages." The key part of his book was a compromise referred to as NOMA, Non Overlapping Magisteria. Of course the non overlap was that Christians were free to preach their creation within the churches while evolutionists and scientists were free to preach their evolution in all other parts of society.

Any attempt to find common ground between Christians and atheist evolutionists is not only doomed to failure, it is absurd. Christians believe in God while evolutionists believe there is no God. How does anyone in their right mind believe a compromise is possible? If some so called Christians believe in only part of God's word, they are questioning their Christian belief. If atheists accept some part of God they are no longer atheists. The atheists are the real hard core evolutionists, and completely control our scientific institutions. They are completely paranoid about

God, or any written literature that would tend to support God, or question Darwinian evolution.

When I was on active duty in the Navy there would, at times, be a disagreement on certain issues. The one thing that probably infuriated me the most, was a senior officer, when faced with differences between subordinates, would try to assume the truth was somewhere between the two sides and look for a compromise. It is completely possible that one side is right and the other side is wrong. Let's face reality. In the case of creation versus evolution, it is becoming more and more clear that science is proving macroevolution impossible. A young earth is proving to be more likely and the age of the earth cannot possibly be in the billions of years, which would be an absolute requirement for Darwinian evolution.

Face it, Darwinian evolution is a fraud. At its origin, prior to appropriate testing, it may have been based on sincere beliefs. In later years however, there has been a conspiracy to hide any scientific facts that deny, or even question, Darwinian evolution. How long does it take to bury a dead concept? It will probably take at least another generation. Most of the scientists today, that control the major scientific establishments, are evolutionists, if not outright atheists. And the scientists that are beginning to see the light on creation are afraid of coming out of the closet. At the present time it seems to be a job ending decision, for a scientist or a teacher, to admit he believes in creation or intelligent design. Some examples are presented in later chapters. Our public schools and the courts are controlled by evolutionists and/or anti-Christians. Many of our churches are too willing to compromise; to look for ways to accept what the atheist scientists tell them, and still retain their Christian beliefs.

As a youth in my home town of Waukesha, Wisconsin, one of my fellow school mates had a father with a nick name of Prof. Ratzin de Garret. He was known for his silly and complex Rube Goldberg type inventions. One of them I remember was a complex cigarette lighter. It involved about ten separate actions. Someone wanting a light would press a button that released a ball bearing. The ball bearing would roll down an incline and hit a small door that would open and release a mouse. The mouse, running down the ramp would set off another action, etc. etc. I don't remember all the intermediate steps, but the final motion moved a match across a piece of sand paper, thus lighting the match to light your cigarette. The point is, every step in this progression was necessary and if one failed the system failed. This was irreducibly complex. But what if someone said, "Not so, I can merely hold the match in my hand and strike it against the sandpaper." That may be true, but irreducible complexity does not mean the same result cannot be obtained by some simpler method or procedure. It simply means that that particular system itself would fail if any single step were removed.

This simple example is used to show the false logic used by Mr. Kenneth Miller in his book where he tries to refute Behe's irreducible complexity. Mr. Miller claims the 9 plus 2 microscopic tubular structure of the cilium presented by Mr. Behe can be simplified and is therefore not irreducibly complex. On page 141 of his book, Mr. Miller stated:

> "A phone call to any biologist who had ever actually studied cilia and flagella would have told Behe that he's wrong in his contention that the 9 + 2 structure is the only way to make a working cilium or flagellum."

Mr. Miller resorts to one of the tactics of the evolutionists by misquoting someone and then proving the quote wrong. Behe never said, or contended, that the 9+2 structure is the only way to make a working cilium. In fact, in several examples, Mr. Behe clearly shows, that some other systems that are irreducibly complex, could still have the same final result met by a simpler, but different system. But the simpler system could never evolve to the more complex.

Mr. Miller goes on to present other cilia with a 9 plus 1 system, a 9 plus 0 system a 6 plus 0 as well as a 3 plus 0 system. All of this may very well be true. But as in the Rube Goldberg example, the cigarette lighter example, and several examples by Mr. Behe, irreducible complexity does not mean there is not a simpler way to achieve the result. It means that particular system is irreducibly complex and the failure of any part means failure for the system. Mr. Miller did not show that any of his simpler systems could evolve to the more complex. The principal point of this entire issue is, can the unbelievably complex cellular structure at the microscopic level all have occurred through random accidental changes? The only real answer is absolutely no. Is Mr. Miller aware of the false logic used in his book? Probably. But does he care? Probably not. Mr. Miller, like Dawkins, Hawking, Gould, Crick and other hard core evolutionists appear to have an agenda. It is to discredit the God of creation, however and whenever possible. And this also means supporting Darwinian evolution at all costs.

While Michael Behe's "Darwin's Black Box" certainly drove the final nail in the Darwinian evolution coffin with his microscopic evidence, he was not the first to point out irreducible complexity. Darwin himself questioned his evolution belief in regards to the human eye. Mr. Miller quotes Darwin on page 135, "To suppose that the eye, with all its inimitable contrivances for adjusting focus to different distances,...could have been formed by natural selection, seems, I freely confess, absurd in the highest possible degree." But then Darwin departs from any scientific concept and resorts to wishful thinking when he also wrote, and it is also quoted by Mr. Miller:

> "Yet reason tells me, that if numerous gradations from a perfect and complex eye to one very imperfect and simple, each grade being useful to its possessor, can be shown to exist; if further, the eye does vary ever so slightly, and the variations be inherited,

which is certainly the case; and if any variation or modification in the organ be ever useful to an animal under changing conditions of life, then the difficulty of believing that a perfect and complex eye could be formed by natural selection, though insuperable by our imagination, can hardly be considered real."

Good Grief! This is nothing but wishful thinking, linking one if to another if, with a few possibles and maybes, thrown in. William Jennings Bryan said it well when he stated Darwin used the phrase "we may well suppose" 800 times in his books. I didn't count them, and it may be an exaggeration, but nothing Darwin had shown scientifically came even close to proving macroevolution. One might ask, how can an intelligent human, especially someone referring to himself as a scientist, accept the fictional drivel by Charles Darwin and reject the scientific evidence presented by Michael Behe? The only answer is a dogmatic atheist faith that is so fixated on opposing the Christian God, that nothing else matters. There should be a line somewhere, where dogmatic, atheist faith, becomes just another word for stupid.

One example of distorted logic, used by an evolutionist to show a universe without design is possible, was by the master of atheistic evolution, Professor Richard Dawkins, in his book "The Blind Watchmaker." Mr. Dawkins states many times in his book, that evolution is completely undirected. Everything happens by pure chance and no intelligence, or planning is allowed.

Mr. Dawkins set up an experiment based on the nebulous belief that, if given enough time, a monkey bashing away at a typewriter, could produce all the works of Shakespeare. Mr. Dawkins simplified this concept, not by using all the works of Shakespeare, but merely the simple phrase, "ME THINKS IT IS LIKE A WEASEL." The sentence had 28 characters in it. Mr. Dawkins' typewriter had a keyboard restricted to 26 capital letters and one space bar. Mr. Dawkins programmed a computer to randomly type a series of 28 characters. To his complete surprise, he never got anything but gibberish. So, being smarter than the average bear, but not by much, he realized the odds against a successful random typing was something like 1 in 10,000 million, million, etc. etc. A really big number. Us peons use the word impossible. So what does a poor defeated atheist do? He fakes it.

Mr. Dawkins merely sneaked a little intelligence into the program. He used the term "cumulative selection" to achieve success. In this case the computer knows in advance what phrase it is looking for.

So when the computer randomly typed a series of letters, the letters that fit in the computer recognized phrase, were saved. The next series would continue and letters that fit in the right place were again saved. Obviously, it didn't take too long for the complete phrase to be typed by the computer.

It seems inconceivable that Mr. Dawkins put intelligence into the computer, but claimed there was no intelligence in his example. To relate this to macroevolution, such as scales to feathers, every cell would have to know in advance what they were looking for. But this would have to ascribe intelligence to the cell and not only that, advance knowledge of what they were trying to evolve to. Mr. Dawkins' failed example is typical of every evolutionist's example that can be proven one way or the other.

There is an intellectual, politically correct, iron curtain around our schools, science organizations, courts, and publishers, that will not permit any questioning of Darwinian evolution. Talk of creation is forbidden. Any information that might support intelligent design is forbidden. It is obvious to all, that intelligent design requires a designer. It is equally obvious to everyone, that the designer is God.

CHAPTER THREE

BEGINNING OF LIFE

As mentioned earlier, the real debate between creation and evolution is misnamed. For living species evolution is further defined as either microevolution or macroevolution. Microevolution is believed by everyone. It has been proven hundreds of times, so it is not even an issue in the controversy. Since it is not an issue and not being contested by anyone, it can't be used as a legitimate argument by either side. If an example of microevolution is used to justify either side, it is intentionally misleading and/or a fraudulent attempt to confuse the issue.

After microevolution is removed as a conflicting issue, we are left with creation vs macroevolution. But before we proceed we must not compare apples with oranges so lets just compare the two beliefs on how life started. Macroevolution has nothing to do with how life started. It only involves how life proceeded after it started. So to be fair, lets compare the Christian belief of how life started with the evolutionist's belief of how life started. So the classic creation-evolution debate has been wrongly argued from the start. You can't legitimately compare creation, which concerns only the start of life, with macroevolution which refers to actions after life started.

Darwin's concept was that one, or a few original single cell organisms evolved into invertebrates, then into fish, then into amphibians, then into reptiles, then into lower mammals, then into primates, then into man. Note that Darwin conveniently, essentially ignores any details of how the spark of life started in these single cell organisms. W.R. Bird, in his two volume set "The Origin of the Species Revisited," Volume I, stated: "The overwhelming supremacy of the myth (Darwin) has created a widespread illusion that the theory of evolution was all but proved one hundred years ago...Nothing could be further from the truth...His general theory is...a highly speculative hypothesis..."

The Exobiology Program within NASA, which studies and searches for extraterrestrial organisms, has adopted the following working definition: "Life is a self sustained chemical system that is capable of undergoing Darwinian, or biological evolution." It would seem ridiculous to define life as something that must be able to perform Darwinian evolution, when the concept has never been proven, has no known examples, and in fact has been proven impossible. Since the words were not defined, perhaps they were referring only to microevolution.

Regardless of NASA's definition I would propose the following definition:

Life: To be alive is to have a God given spark of life. To be able to obtain food and continue life. To be able to reproduce like off springs to perpetuate the species. To perform in life as God has ordained for your species.

God must be laughing and crying at the same time. Laughing at our stupidity in believing all his miracles of creation could have just happened by chance – and crying over the results of the human race that is inevitably rushing towards self destruction.

The Christian belief of how life started is simple and straight forward. It is clearly stated in the first few chapters of Genesis. Some parts of the Bible may not be easy for everyone to comprehend, and in many places God's word involves parables or obvious exaggerations, to make a point. For example, in Matthew, chapter 18, verse 22, Jesus said, in responding to Peter, you should forgive your brother "70 times 7." Of course he did not mean you should keep score and after 490 offenses you no longer need to forgive.

But in the creation account nothing could be worded more simply and clearly. How can anyone misinterpret "In the beginning God created the heaven and the earth?" Or, in verse 11, "And God said Let the earth bring forth grass, the herb yielding seed, and the fruit tree yielding fruit after his kind, whose seed is in itself, upon the earth: and it was so."

So the creation belief is fairly straight forward. Anyone that refuses to understand or believe the simplicity and clearness of the creation account in the Bible, denies the obvious and does so for some ulterior motive. But how do evolutionists claim life started? There is no real consensus, but we will consider some of the evolutionists' writings. And, of course most if not all of these weird beliefs are supported, not by scientific facts, but by our scientific establishments.

In his book "Aquagenesis, the origin and evolution of life in the sea", author Richard Ellis attempts to show all life started from non-life, and then proceeded thru many macroevolution steps to create all the denizens of the deep, and more. Even before his preface he quoted Erasmus Darwin from "the Temple of Nature", 1802:

> "Hence without parents, by spontaneous birth
> Rise the first specks of animated earth....
> Organic life beneath the shoreless waves
> Was born and nurs'd in ocean's pearly caves;
> First forms minute, unseen by spheric glass,
> Move on the mud, or pierce the watery mass;
> These, as successive generations bloom,
> New powers acquire and larger limbs assume
> Whence countless groups of vegetation
> spring, And breathing realms of fin and feet and wing."

This is an interesting poem as science fiction but has no credibility in science and does not even support being referred to as a hypothesis, much less theory. In over 200 years since this poem was written, scientists still have no better information on how life started. Our present evolutionist scientists still believe life started by spontaneous generation in some pre-historic pond, or ocean, or whatever. Our present evolutionist scientists also believe in the Biogenesis theory that states all life comes from existing life. Can you say hypocrite?

Mr. Ellis' book is admittedly for those that "...do not believe that God made everything on earth in the first six actual days." His entire book then, is based on the assumption that there is no God, and everything had to happen naturally.

Mr. Ellis stated "there may have been a fortuitous combination of elements and conditions in the primeval ocean that more or less accidentally created life." He also claimed that a graduate student formulated a theory that life had originated in the Archean Period, about 4.2 billion years ago, on the sea floor..." Anyone can formulate an hypothesis, which is nothing more than a scientist's guess, but to go beyond hypothesis to theory, that requires some evidence. None exists.

"Science"-Fiction:

Life begins with one cell in the ocean

"OK, I've formed by accident. Life from non-life! Now all I have to do is not die right away until I can figure out how to reproduce and then over time become fish and reptiles and amphibians and insects and birds and mammals and then humans!"

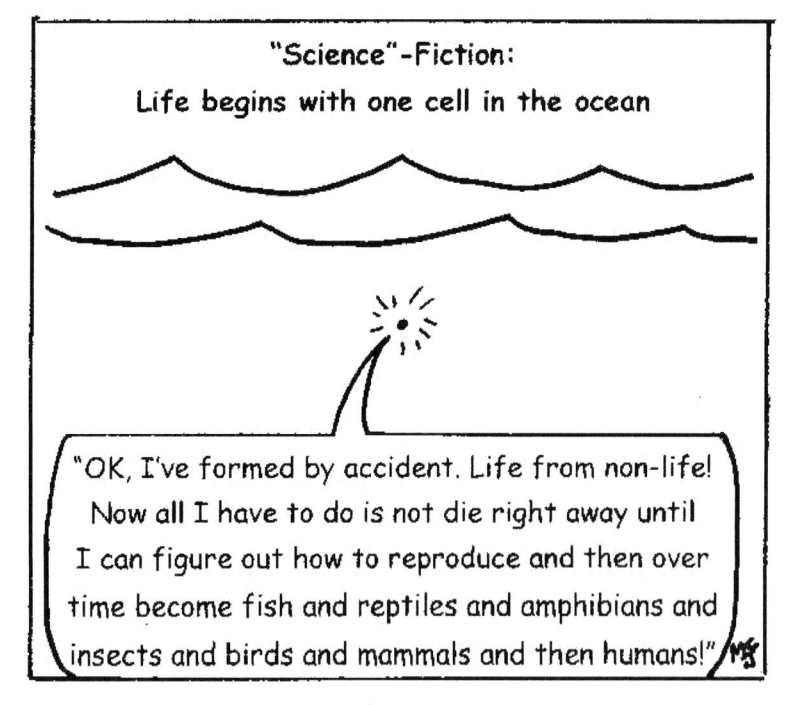

Figure 1

Mr. Ellis also claimed "The unique conditions around subterranean hydrothermal vents made them strong candidates for a deep-ocean location of the origin of life." Mr. Ellis also referred to a water depth of 8,200 feet in the Galapagos Rift Zone of the eastern Pacific, where hydrothermal vents are cracks in the sea floor at the junction of two tectonic plates. Volcanic gasses are acclaimed to heat the water to temperatures of nearly 700 degrees F. And Viola! Life can form. What real evidence is there that this happened, or could happen? Can you say none, or zero? With no supporting evidence whatsoever, this belief or scientific guess cannot even be substantiated as a hypothesis. Why would anyone believe this? Because atheists will accept anything, no matter how absurd, if it denies God.

There are many other beliefs of how life started without God. None of them go beyond mere speculation. One biology book states "The origin of life is unknown. Many scientists believe life arose spontaneously...." A popular high school biology book, "Biological Science" BSCS Blue Version, 7th edition, lists four possible ideas as to how life could have started on earth.

1. Life originated by unknown means
2. Life originated by unknown means outside earth.
3. Life was created by a supernatural force or deity.
4. Life evolved from non-living matter

Of course the book immediately discredits creation by saying: "it does not have a scientific basis." What kind of confused logic would accept the other three as having a scientific basis? Of course the concept of spontaneous generation, involved in all the other beliefs, defies the basic genetic law that all life comes from existing life. But double standards are normal for evolutionists, and in fact, necessary.

While there are probably many dozens of books and articles that try to explain the origin of life without God, make no mistake, there is not a shred of scientific evidence to support any of them. The only common ground in all of these spontaneous generation of life beliefs, is the atheistic assumption that there is no God. But life itself is a miracle. It is not a product of the natural but of the super natural.

I have recently reviewed several books by evolutionists and find they are all pretty much in agreement on how life started; in some unknown prehistoric pond or ocean, in some unknown manner, and for some unknown reason that they can't explain. They only know it happened. Conclusions first – evidence later (maybe). Mr. George Ellis attempted to clarify the subject a little in his book "Before the Beginning, Cosmology Explained." Mr. Ellis first puts creation in its place by stating:

> "...the theological view has been forced to retreat abandoning to science much previously claimed territory...large move away from religion on the part of thinking men and women..." Mr. Ellis goes on to say: "All the evidence points to a process of evolution whereby single cell animals developed out of carbon-based molecules thousands or millions of years ago, and then evolved to higher and higher levels of complexity, culminating in the existence of the human race. This is supported both by the fossil record...and evolution taking place in populations of flies, bacteria, viruses and animals (dog breeding and horse breeding)......recently acquired evidence ..where embryos of humans and of many animals are found to be virtually indistinguishable for the first few weeks of their growth....the historical occurrence of evolution is beyond reasonable doubt...the nature of mechanisms...to account for this process...is still open to debate."

Mr. Ellis' comments on the start of life and evolution, is typical; conclusions first-evidence later (maybe). With all of his high tech knowledge and comments, Mr. Ellis resorts to examples of microevolution as proof of evolution and Haeckel's long discredited belief that embryos of humans and animals are indistinguishable for the first few weeks of growth. Why do intelligent people make such idiotic comments? Of course all embryos are alike in their physical appearance. At the beginning, they all look something like the period at the end of this sentence. But the genetic information within the embryo is as different as day and night. Mr. Ellis, like all evolutionists, start with the dogmatic belief that science is their god. With that kind of mental blinders, they may never see truth. Conclusions first, evidence later, maybe.

In the comic strip, Non Sequitur, the little girl, Danae, is wise beyond her years. In a recent comic strip she explained to Lucy, her horse friend, that she is a preconceptual scientist. A scientist that reaches a conclusion to a theory first, then just ignores all evidence to prove it wrong. And with no evidence to prove it wrong, it must be right. Doesn't this sound familiar? Could the scientists at the National Academy of Sciences have discovered the preconceptual scientist concept, first?

Not to continue beating a dead horse, but this is a true story. A few years ago, when I went to the barber shop, I noticed a few grey hairs on the apron. I had never before noticed my hair turning grey. I look into the mirror every day when I comb my hair and really never noticed any grey hair. This continued for several years. I never noticed my hair turning grey until I went to the barber shop to get a haircut. The cuttings on the apron were getting more and more grey. I am kind of slow at times, but it finally hit me. My barber was turning my hair grey. Well, I never went back to that barber again. But it was too late, my hair was almost white.

I am not aware of any real evidence I can come up with, except every time I got my hair cut it was more grey than the time before. That is good enough for me. My obvious conclusion was that the barber was turning my hair grey. I am looking for other evidence to prove my barber was guilty of turning my hair grey. Others have tried to offer contrary evidence, they say is true, in an attempt to show the grey hair might be caused by something else. But I am no fool. Any contrary evidence would be counter to my final conclusion that the barber is guilty. Obviously, I cannot permit that kind of evidence.

If evolutionists can deny any evidence contrary to their belief in Darwinian evolution then I should be able to reject any evidence contrary to my final pre-determined conclusion. Truth denied is truth denied, no matter the reason. The barber must be guilty.

While scientists have never been able to identify how life started, they are hard at work in trying to create life. After all, if life started on its own some time in the ancient past, then surely our scientists, with all their knowledge, should be able to repeat the start of life.

A recent Associated Press release in the Washington Times, on August 20th, 2007, reported that, "Scientists Race to Invent Artificial Life." One of the leaders in the field, Jack Szostak, at Harvard Medical School, "predicts that within the next six months, scientists will report evidence that the first step—creating a cell membrane—is not a big problem." So in six months a report will merely say, "its not a big problem." Big Deal. The cell membrane, while certainly complex, and it is alive, is simplicity itself when compared to the inner workings of a living cell.

Several authors have described the inner workings of a cell as equivalent to a complete walled city, with roads, buildings, factories, gates, doors, etc. Every component is alive and performing its own assigned function. The microscopic complexity is almost beyond our imagination. One thing the scientists, trying to create life don't say, is where they will get the one ingredient they can't make – the God given spark of life. All of the scientist's current experiments on creating new life, start with an existing living cell, or living components. Without that critical, God given spark of life, they can create nothing. But the evolutionists keep trying.

I have discussed earlier that microevolution, believed and accepted by everyone, is no longer part of the debate. That leaves only macroevolution for the evolutionists to argue and support. And on the other side of the debate, creation, I have shown, is to be compared only with the evolutionist's belief of how life started. So creation is removed from the debate with evolution concerning how life progressed after it started. Macroevolution then stands naked and alone, and can gain no support by any attempted false comparison with any religious belief. The only real controversy then, is macroevolution against truth.

What an enormous change in the classic creation-evolution debate. Macroevolution must stand alone against truth. So called evolution can no longer attempt to gain credibility by claiming it is science while creation is religion. It can not gain support by discrediting religion. It must stand on its own against truth. And the major goal of this book is to show that macroevolution not only fails the truth test, it is, and has always been, a total lie.

The British Government issued a white paper in December 2006, that called for a ban on what they called "interspecies embryos ". But the ban was just the opposite. It did not ban, but provided exceptions that permitted research into embryos that were part human and part animal. Part of the discussion was how to classify a creature that was 50% human and 50% animal. To think the scientists are even discussing such a thing is disgusting.

Evolution cannot explain, and in fact denies, the sharp line between humans, made in God's image, and animals. Language and the written word were given to us by God so we could better communicate with him. We have a God given sense of morality that animals don't have. Humans have a soul, the ability to think, to plan, to love, to hate, to worship the Lord they know as their creator, and for those who accept God, to look forward to a life hereafter in eternity. Animals have none of these attributes but were created for mankind's use and pleasure. This is all clear in the Bible and there has never been any scientific evidence to the contrary.

Another true story. I have discovered that gold rings shrink over a long period of time-like 55 years or so. I don't know the cause of this. I only know it is true. Very few of you reading this, have worn a gold ring for 55 years, so you are in no position to disagree. For many years I could easily remove my gold wedding ring when I wished to. In recent years it became more and more difficult to remove the ring. I would estimate that there was no noticeable shrinkage for the first 50 years. Recently the ring has become so tight that it is impossible go get it past the first knuckle. It should be obvious to anyone that the gold ring is shrinking. There are some that want to question my pre-conceived conclusion. But I can't allow any such evidence that would be counter to my conclusions that the ring is shrinking. I am following the evolutionist's concept of conclusions first-evidence later. I am thinking of sending a warning to all senior citizens that may be wearing a gold ring. Makes sense to me.

Buddy Davis is a song writer and ballad singer with Answers in Genesis. He has written many songs based on Christianity and creation in particular. He is very popular with both young and old. One of my favorites is copied below. (too bad you can't hear me singing it)

> "If there really was a world wide flood,
> What would the evidence be?
> Billions of dead things,
> Buried in rock layers,
> Laid down by water,
> All over the Earth."

And what do we find? Exactly that. Billions of dead fossils, buried in rock layers, laid down by water in sedimentary layers, all over the Earth. Sounds convincing to me. But there is more.

Evolution depends on what they call uniformitarianism. The present is the key to the past. So what is happening in the present that would explain all the fossils? Can you say nothing? Sedimentary rock layers laid down by water are sometimes hundreds of feet thick. They all had to be laid down in a fairly short time period for two reasons. The first is that these sedimentary rock layers, in many places, contain a very drastic curvature which indicate they had to be completely formed while the layers were still pliable. Did you ever try to bend a rock? The second reason they had to be formed in a relatively short period of time, is the appearance of polystrate fossils. These are petrified tree trunks extending vertically through many layers of the strata. Obviously the tree trunk could not have existed and remained vertical for thousands of years while the sediment built up around it. But there is more.

Marine fossils are found near the tops of all the mountains. Wow! How did they get there? Who put them there? Dr. Francis Crick, co-discoverer of the DNA molecule, and a highly respected scientist could say, as he did about life starting on earth, (page 2) they came from outer space. Well that would explain how they got to the tops of the mountains, but Dr Crick has one fatal flaw in everything he says. He is an admitted atheist and they have this unwritten law that no atheist can ever question the fact of Darwinian evolution. If they did, they would be kicked out of the atheist camp and probably get fired as well. Who would have thought that if you want to find marine fossils, go mountain climbing.

But seriously, how did marine fossils get to the tops of the mountains? Most evolutionists say, "no problem." The fossils were well established on the mountains when the Earth was flat. They don't really mean flat. They knew the Earth was always round, but without mountains. Noah's flood would not have required as much water if there were no mountains. If the mountains were once flat, or at least below sea level they could have collected all those fossils . and then, Viola! The mountains raised up. Some as high as 15,000 to 20,000 feet or more. And this all over the Earth.

The only problem with this is the evolutionists deny any catastrophe and believe the present is the key to the past. How many of you have seen, or read lately, of a mountain rising up to great heights from below sea level? The rapid build up of sedimentary rock and the marine fossils near the tops of the mountains, cry out, catastrophe.

Does it really matter whether the mountains were covered with water before or after they rose to their present heights? Macroevolution is impossible, so it really doesn't matter, in the big debate, whether the mountains rose with the fossils or the fossils collected after the mountains reached their present height. Either way, the fossils were collected underwater, and this was a world wide event.

CHAPTER FOUR

MICROEVOLUTION & MACROVOLUTION

It has always amazed me that intelligent individuals in the evolution controversy are either not aware of, or totally ignore, the stark difference between micro and macroevolution. It is a major difference whether only existing genetic information is available in an offspring, or whether new genetic information is introduced. Why would any intelligent person, knowing the difference, attempt to merely lump the two together in any presentation? So for evolutionists to use examples of microevolution to support their Darwinian evolution is disingenuous at best.

A clear understanding of micro and macroevolution and how the terms are intentionally corrupted by evolutionists will be a defacto coup d'e-tat that will destroy the Darwinian belief. Why? Because nearly every example scientists present to support evolution is merely microevolution. Not one of the many books and articles by evolutionists that I have seen, clearly explain, or specifically discuss, micro and macroevolution. Everyone believes in microevolution. Since everyone believes in microevolution it cannot be a party to any conflict between evolutionists and creationists. So it would make more sense to totally exclude all references to microevolution in any discussion. If evolutionists believe that enough minor changes, over a long enough period of time, could lead to macroevolution changes, then they should provide only the specific changes involved. This they do not do, because they don't have any.

A few years ago, some students, while trying to prove a point, or perhaps merely as a stunt, sought signatures on a petition from passers by outside a local market. The petition was to ban the use of dihydrogen oxide, since, as the petition clearly stated, it was the single greatest cause of children's deaths every summer. Most patrons were willing to sign the petition without knowing, or caring what dihydrogen oxide was. They just knew it was bad.

Of course dihydogen oxide (H20) is merely the chemical identification of water. Whether drowning is in fact the single greatest cause of child deaths in the summer is irrelevant. This is a perfect example of how people can be hood winked into falling for nebulous or misleading arguments. Evolutionists use similar logic in supporting their false views. The continuous use of the word evolution, without specifying whether they are referring to micro or macroevolution is a good example.

The disingenuous attempt to portray obvious examples of microevolution as macroevolution, and then claim evolution has been proven, is the norm for evolutionists. While an entire book could be written just discussing these fraudulent examples, only a few will be identified to reveal the concept.

Mr. Ashley Montagu, edited a book, "Science and Creationism" which contained a series of essays, including one by Stephen Jay Gould. In his essay Mr. Gould clearly recognized the difference between micro and macroevolution but he attempted to minimize the difference. He stated:

> "Our confidence that evolution occurred centers upon three general arguments. First, we have abundant, direct, observational evidence of evolution in action, both from the field and laboratory. It ranges from countless experiments on change in nearly everything about fruit flies subjected to artificial selection in the laboratory, to the famous British moths that turned black when industrial soot darkened the trees upon which they rest."

It is obvious, of course, that all of Gould's examples to support his first argument are merely microevolution; minor changes within the same species. We can forgive Gould for not being aware that the British moth situation was a fraud, since at the time he wrote the above, the fraud had not been discovered. So what are the other two arguments Mr. Gould presents to prove evolution? He goes on to state:

"The second and third arguments-the case for major changes, (macroevolution) do not involve direct observation of evolution in action. They rest upon inference but are no less secure for that reason."

Good grief! The only proof offered then for macroevolution, by Mr. Gould's own words, rests on inferences. And they call this a scientific fact? The most widely publicized species associated with Darwin's name are the Galapagos' finches, with their different beak sizes and shapes. Everything Darwin reported about these finches was absolutely true. But what he didn't say was that all the changes he discovered, with his finches and every other species he investigated, involved microevolution only. Darwin found no evidence that the finches ever evolved to another species, or that they evolved from another species.

It seems almost incredible that all of Darwin's studies, experiments and research involved microevolution only. The concept that over a long period of time, minor changes, or microevolution, would lead to major changes, or macroevolution, is without any scientific supporting evidence. Darwinian evolution is not a fact as many claim, it is not even a legitimate theory. It is merely a hypothesis with no scientific evidence to raise it to the status of a theory.

The biology book "Living, An introduction to biology" by Melissa Stanley & George Andrykovitch is typical of most in their evolution comments. They stated,

"mutations are rare and usually lethal. Occasionally, however, under the prevailing conditions, a mutation can be harmless or even beneficial".

However, no legitimate examples are given here, or anywhere, of a truly beneficial mutation. The authors also state:

> "Although most of the history of life can only be inferred, sometimes we can observe evolution directly. English moth collectors have documented a tiny but telling example of evolution in the peppered moth."

Without going into irrelevant details, the black and white peppered moth story involved moths changing from being mostly white to mostly black because of an environment change. This example has appeared in most biology books in the past and you will probably still find it in current books. The entire peppered moth saga has been a fiasco from the start. Even if true, it was always only microevolution and more recently was discovered to be a fraud as well.

The authors also make the claim, as do many others, that: "The theory of evolution is the single most unifying idea within biology. It explains not only the similarities in the chemistry and structure of organisms, but also their marked diversity."

Is the theory of evolution the most unifying idea within biology? I don't know whether the author is referring to microevolution or macroevolution. If the author is referring to microevolution, then it would certainly be considered an important part of biology. The study of genetic and inherited traits is a very important part of biology. But then we have macroevolution, which, has yet to come up with a single example, has no basis in science, and has been shown to be impossible. What scientist could possibly claim this to be an important biological concept?

An interesting side light in the biology book lists over thirty scientists and doctors from 300 B.C. to 1970 that have made important contributions to the advance of biology. How many of these do you think supported macroevolution?

Charles Darwin was the only one listed and he provided no scientific evidence for macroevolution.

Speciation is defined as the evolution of a new species through time. The classic example given in many biology books, consists of a species of animals that become divided by a flood, or some other natural occurrence, and the two sections are kept apart through many generations. If they could then reunite, they may no longer be able to interbreed. So it is alleged we have a new species.

Some evolution writers also claim speciation can also be artificially caused or manipulated. The fruit fly is given as a candidate that has been tinkered with by scientists using radiation and various other means. Many different, and I might say crippled, fruit flies have been the result. In most cases the fruit flies ended up with extra wings, deformed wings, extra legs and other deformities. None ever changed from being a fruit fly. Can you say, microevolution?

Other examples of speciation given in some biology books involve the separation of the squirrels on both sides of the Grand Canyon, some birds that seem almost identical but can't interbreed, a type of desert lizard and others. All of the examples given are merely microevolution or really devolution.

Darwin and the evolutionists approach the issue improperly. They first assume there is no God. They then assume that all life had to start and proceed to its present status all by natural means. They then look for evidence to support that belief. All evidence available is bent, twisted or misinterpreted to conform to their pre-determined conclusion. This is obvious from one of their claims that they know evolution occurred, they just might not know the exact form it took. In the meantime any evidence to the contrary is denied. It wouldn't get past an atheist peer review.

But again, speciation does not introduce any new genetic information. For Darwinian evolution, or macroevolution, we need new genetic information to allow for any upward evolution. These examples given for speciation involve the loss of genetic information. If anything this would be called de-evolution, just the opposite of macroevolution. At best, speciation would result in a sub-species. It is not an example of Darwinian evolution as the books imply.

The basic conflict between creation and evolution has been miss-handled for years. We should compare the Christian belief of origins with the Secular Humanist belief of origins. And we should compare one belief of how life progressed after it started, with the other belief of how life progressed after it started. Creation, the Christian belief of how life started, should then be compared to the Darwinian belief that life started in some pre-historic pond or ocean, in some unexplainable way, or miracle that cannot be explained by any known science today. Concerning Darwinian evolution then, or how life progressed after it started, there is nothing on the Christian side to compare it to. Life did not progress to new species beyond God's initial creation. Evolution, properly defined, must include microevolution and macroevolution. Microevolution, or minor changes within a species, is an obvious and known fact, and is widely accepted by everyone without question. Therefore it should be removed from any controversy.

That leaves the only controversy about how life progressed up to macroevolution, with nothing to compare it to, except truth. Did macroevolution happen? The entire conflict then, on how life progressed, should be macroevolution against truth. It is up to the Darwinian evolutionists to prove it. And this they have been unable to do.

Evolutionists frequently say the key to evolution is natural selection. But this is false. Why? Because natural selection is the same as survival of the fittest. They are not just equal, and to use a geometry term, they are congruent. That is to say, identical. An example is two rabbits running for their life when being chased by a fox. The fastest will get away, and whatever is in his genetic makeup that makes him fast, will be passed on to his off spring. An animal with the thickest fur will better survive an unusually cold winter.

This also explains the obvious minor changes in the beak shapes of Darwin's Galapagos finches. These are examples of natural selection and survival of the fittest. Survival of the fittest then, is microevolution in action. It is obvious to everyone and not an issue. But what evidence is there to indicate these minor changes could ever lead to macroevolution changes? Absolutely none.

CHAPTER FIVE

MISSING LINKS

The search for missing links has become a fetish with paleontologists. What a shame. So many careers are involved. It is like hiring dozens of highly paid workers to look for the proverbial needle in a haystack, but don't tell them there isn't any needle there. Macroevolution has already been proven impossible. There won't be any missing links found since they never existed. But according to the evolution philosophy of conclusions first – evidence later we will continue to look for the non existent. To be truthful, most atheist evolutionists probably don't really care. They are primarily interested in keeping the anti-Christian efforts going.

In past years several alleged missing links were found and given much publicity. But alas, all that could be really identified were discredited. A pig's tooth did not become Nebraska Man, monkey skulls from Peking were lost at sea and a filed and stained head bone affectionately named Piltdown man turned out to be an intentional fraud. But Piltdown man served the evolutionists well. He had everyone fooled for forty years. Other well known candidates for the missing link include Java Man, Lucy and a bunch of assorted skulls. In every case where it could be positively identified, all were either fully human or fully ape. There is no in between.

In the search for missing links, I don't know whether we should laugh or cry. Not a single verified, true missing link, has been discovered between any two species. If macroevolution were true, there would necessarily be at least hundreds of thousands, if not millions of intermediate life forms. In fact, there would be far more intermediate forms than there are species. There would be so many you wouldn't be able to tell where a cat ended and a dog began, or whatever.

SIAMESE BULL CAT*

*A cross between a Siamese Cat and a Bull Dog. Fortunately it's fictional - Just like macro-evolution!

Figure 2

Evolutionists claim a few missing links in the maritime kingdom as well. A fossil of a large fish called a coelacanth was found and dated to be 70 million years old. In 1938 some fishermen near Madagascar, not knowing the fish had long been extinct, caught some. They admitted later they had been catching them for years. What made this fish so important were the four fins on the bottom that had been scheduled by the evolutionists to grow into legs, and feet, and walk out of the water. The creature was scheduled to become an amphibian and then a true land animal. How do we know this? We know evolution is true so it must have happened. This is in agreement with the evolution philosophy of conclusions first-evidence later.

A VERY FISHY STORY

"Hmmm, I want to move to land, so I guess I need to develop lungs. Now I have no idea what lungs are, but I'm sure if I just close my eyes and wish real hard, I can grow some!"

Figure 3

Another area where the search for missing links is still active is the dinosaur to bird transition. This is not just a belief, it is a fact. How do we know this? We know this because birds and dinosaurs have three toes. The first bird-dino missing link was called pro-avis. Now pro-avis never existed, even as a fossil. It was only a drawing but since it is a known fact that dinos evolved into birds, it had to have existed. It was just waiting to be found.

One of the favorite bird intermediates today is archaeopteryx, whose fossil remains were found in Germany in the late 1860's. Claimed to be a feathered reptile, it has come under continuing attack by creationists and evolutionists alike. The skeleton seems to be exactly like that of a small running dinosaur, the comsognathus, but with feathers. There is some evidence that the feathered impressions were added to the only two fossils that show feathers. Walt Brown in his book "In the Beginning: Compelling Evidence for Creation and the Flood" claims that since the early 1980s several prominent scientists have charged the feather impressions were a forgery. Does it really matter? Macroevolution has already been proven impossible. Concern over archaeopteryx is akin to worrying whether your bald tire will be able to finish your trip, in the middle of the desert, after your engine just blew up.

But there is more. Recent findings coming from China have added new information to the dino-bird issue. The November 1999 issue of National Geographic magazine featured a dinosaur-bird missing link. The following is quoted from a USA Today article by Tim Friend:

> "From the remote Liaoning Province of China, an unusual dinosaur fossil has made a mysterious journey from the hands of Chinese smugglers to the polished halls of the National Geographic Societyin Washington. And like some curse from a mummy's tomb, the archaeoraptor, supposedly a bird like creature with the tail of a meat eating dinosaur, has been brought to those who would possess it what may be remembered as modern paleontology's greatest embarrassment."

The article goes on to explain the fossil was a composite of two fossils intentionally combined to appear as one. The National Geographic described it as a true missing link in the complex chain that connects dinosaurs to birds.(three toes-it had to be a link) But a later deceit will probably top this one. An Associated Press article on Feb. 12, 2003, concerned a find in China of a four winged dinosaur that glided from tree to tree. When this is discredited a new fossil will come along to take its place.

The only issue with the evolutionists is not whether dinosaurs evolved into birds but whether they did it from the ground up, or from the trees down.

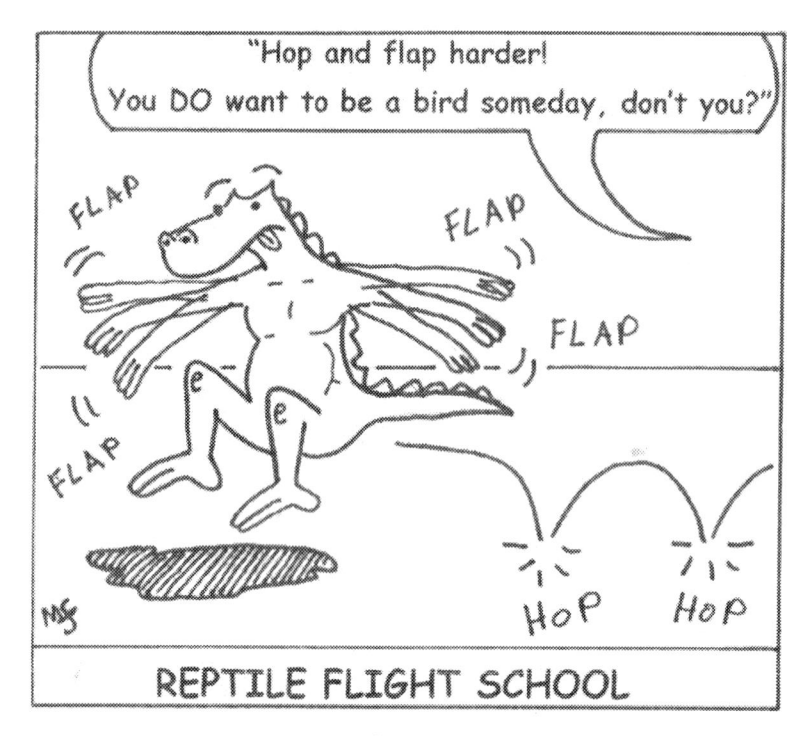

Figure 4

This is a major contention. Talk about an argument of fools. Some evolutionists believe the dinosaurs ran along the ground and jumped up while waving their arms or front legs, or whatever. Eventually the front legs evolved into wings with feathers and we have a bird. Not so say others. The dinosaurs climbed trees and leaped off into space waving their front arms or legs, whatever. Eventually the front legs grew feathers and evolved into wings. We know this happened because we start out with the conclusions and fill in the details later. If any one is reading this information for the first time, I assure you I am not making this up. If you could see me, I am holding up my right hand in the Boy Scout oath, which is better than having it notarized.

A recent book, published in 2005, "Smithsonian Intimate Guide to Human Origins" by Carl Zimmer, is typical of both evolutionist's publications and the

Smithsonian's atheist base. Origins should refer to a starting point, but this is conveniently overlooked, since the evolutionists don't really have a starting point. The book does nothing more than present a bunch of ancient bones and parts of skulls, in various stages of decomposition, and then tries to arrange them in some sort of evolutionary order. The book is a farce since macroevolution, the real main ingredient of Darwinian evolution, is ignored. The book assumes that there is no God, that natural selection is the key, and that minor changes in a species can lead to a new species. Mr. Zimmer stated:

> "Experts today agree that Darwin's basic idea was both brilliant and sound. All the evidence supports the hypothesis that our ancestors evolved from quadrupeds into bipeds."

Of course this is true if you are referring to atheist experts. But in the real world, there is no proof that any species ever evolved into a more advanced species. A bunch of ancient skulls and bones, in various stages of decomposition doesn't prove anything. Macroevolution is not scientifically possible.

Mr. Zimmer also makes the frequent argument that apes didn't evolve to humans because they both separated from some ancient species and evolved along different, but parallel paths. The entire argument is both trivial and irrelevant. If macroevolution were true, there would be no celebration or hero worship over a single so called missing link. There would be so many intermediates, no one single intermediate would get more attention than the thousands of others.

The creation belief has been gaining considerable ground and support through many new books and new scientific discoveries. A new, first class, multi- million dollar creation museum, built by Answers in Genesis (AiG), near Cincinnati Ohio, is having tremendous success in bringing the truth of the Biblical account of creation to the public.

Probably in response to the growing support for creation, the evolutionists are fighting back. A recent Associated Press release claimed that "Lucy", the evolutionist's bones of a so called missing link, left Ethiopia for Texas and will go on display in a Houston museum. This is part of a tour of U.S. museums to support the fading Darwinian belief. Lucy, one of the Australopithecus fossils, is the queen bee of missing links. But one might wonder, if macroevolution were true, there would necessarily be hundreds of thousands, if not millions of missing links found, and all would be equally important. The fact that only one is worshipped instead of the many thousands, is a clear indication that there aren't any real intermediate life forms. Lucy is nothing more than the bones of a dead ape. Can you say fraud?

CHAPTER SIX

CONSPIRACY OF THE SCIENTISTS

There is no doubt that Darwinian evolution is the most politically correct, and well established belief in the country. All our public schools, universities, the public media, and even many churches worship at the feet of Charles Darwin. No biology book could get accepted in our public schools if it even questioned the sacred Darwinian evolution belief. Some educators and scientists have lost their jobs for merely questioning some of the Darwinian concepts. Peer review, required by the scientific community before a scientific paper can be published, is a joke. On any controversial subject, if the reviewers are all on the one side of the issue, we don't have peer review, we have censorship.

A good example of how false, but politically correct beliefs, by the so called favored few, can over ride real evidence is revealed in the recent book by M. Stanton Evans, "Blacklisted by History." This is a very detailed and thoroughly researched book on how Senator Joseph McCarthy, in the 1950's, was treated by the government politicians. In his book, Mr. Evans stated:

> "That there was a wide ranging high-level plot consisting of multiple Alger Hisses, as alleged by McCarthy, was for many in influential places, too preposterous for belief. It was either a smear, or paranoia, or a quest for unworthy headlines, or something, but couldn't possibly be the truth. It was in a word, unthinkable—unthinkable that such a plot existed, or that the people named by McCarthy could be complicit in such betrayal... His targets, often as not, were Ivy League respectable types in the mold of Hiss or Duggan. How could one believe such

outlandish charges from such a lout, aimed at his social betters? One couldn't, and one didn't."

The first evidence concerning Communists in high level government positions was known to the FBI in the 1930's and presented to other government agencies in 1939. But it was over ten years later before any real action was taken. Mr. Evans quotes from a memo in the FBI files, to Hoover, by Chief Special Agent Guy Hottel, in March 1946:

> "It has become increasingly clear in the investigation of this case that there are a tremendous number of persons employed in the United States government who are Communists and strive daily to advance the cause of Communism and destroy the foundations of this government....Today nearly every department or agency of this government is infiltrated with them in varying degree."

Final, overwhelming factual evidence, proved without any doubt that Senator McCarthy was correct in his claim of many Communists in high government positions. All of Senator McCarthy's information came from State Department, or FBI documents. But to this day, Almost sixty years later, the name of McCarthy is still discredited by many uninformed Americans and the so called politically correct media. .

Similarly, our premier science organization in the country, The National Academy of Sciences, continues to ride rough shod over truth in their continuing denial of legitimate evidence that opposes their dogmatic belief in Darwinian evolution. Anyone challenging Darwinian evolution, or even suggesting that Intelligent Design is a legitimate possibility, will not find his evidence challenged, but he himself will be vilified and ostracized in the politically correct, scientific community.

How did this great nation, founded by Christians, and with a constitution, government, and laws, based solidly on

Christian moral values, degenerate to its present status? This chapter will deal primarily with the semi-government agency that bears much of the responsibility, The National Academy of Sciences (NAS). According to their web site:

> "The National Academy of Sciences (NAS) is an honorific society of distinguished scholars engaged in scientific and engineering and research...The NAS was signed into being by President Abraham Lincoln on March 3, 1863...to investigate, examine, experiment and report upon any subject of science or art whenever called upon to do so by any department of the government."

Some relatively new terms have been introduced into the discussion in order to clarify some of the issues. These are, operational science and historical science. We are more familiar with operational science. It concerns present day issues that will meet the requirements for factual science. For example, gravity can be identified, quantified, measured, tested and repeated. Historical science is merely a belief, of what is determined to have happened in the past, based on present day evidence. Obviously it can not be repeated and is based on several assumptions and beliefs.

I have explained earlier that microevolution is not a conflicting issue, since it is widely accepted by everyone. Creation is not an issue except to compare the Christian belief in creation with the evolutionist's belief in spontaneous generation of life. We can really prove neither. The only thing for evolutionists to prove is that macroevolution has occurred.

The definition of science in Webster's First American Dictionary of the English Language, published in 1828, included the words "truth" and "God". In 1978 the NAS published a resolution that stated:

> "...the search for knowledge and understanding of the physical universe and of living things that inhabit

it should be conducted under conditions of intellectual freedom, without religious, political or ideological restrictions... those who challenge existing theory must be protected from retaliatory actions."

Now this sounded great and involved a search for truth no matter where the truth may lie. Anyone was free to challenge existing theories without the fear of any retaliation. This is the way the organization had operated since its founding in 1863. But the search for truth was not to continue. The Academy changed from a basic science organization to a basic atheist organization that would not accept any scientific evidence if it supported Christianity or denied Darwinian evolution.

In 1984, the NAS published a booklet titled "Science and Creationism, A View from the National Academy of Sciences." This booklet made a 180 degree turn in its objectivity. An unapologetic search for truth changed to an atheist search for truth. The creation-evolution debate was settled in the minds of the scientists by definition, and the atheists were the winners.

The 1984 booklet is almost a masterpiece of deceit, falsehoods, misrepresentations and anti-Christian rhetoric. The National Academy of Sciences and the Supreme Court are the two organizations primarily responsible for forcing the lie of evolution on the nation, and in destroying our Christian base.

In spite of the evolutionist's nearly total control of the sciences and the media, the public was still not convinced. With a growing concern over the failure to convince most people about evolution, the NAS published another book in 1998, "Teaching about evolution and the Nature of Science". While there are too many discrepancies, errors and plain misleading facts in both of the documents to cover all of them, some will be exposed to show the fraudulent basis for the books.

This chapter will deal primarily with the semi-government agency (NAS) that, under the guise of science, has taken a leading role is destroying this nation's Godly foundation. The two publications listed above will be shown to be replete with erroneous information and misleading and irrelevant facts that are distorted in order to support the atheist belief in Darwinian evolution. Remember that we are not comparing creation in any way since that has nothing to do with how life progressed, but we are only comparing macroevolution with truth. It may sound incredulous to the average reader, that our leading scientific establishment would put a dogmatic atheist belief ahead of its scientific search for truth, but for the skeptics I would only say, read on.

The two documents by the NAS use several misleading concepts to support their atheist arguments. Once these are pointed out, and one is aware of them, the truth becomes evident. The first misleading concept is to present an example of something that is completely true and associate it with evolution, while presenting something that is obviously false, and associate it with creation. While in fact neither have anything to do with the issue. The below quote is from the first NAS booklet:

> "Before you begin to read this discussion of science and creationism, please take a careful look at the front and back cover of this book. The front cover depicts the earth as we know it today. (a picture of earth taken from outer space) The back cover Illustrates the world as the people believed it to be, in the days before Columbus sailed to the new world. (a crude distorted drawing of the world as depicted 500 years ago)... One belongs to the world as we have come to know it and the other belongs in history."

The point of this is obviously to associate creation with an outdated concept, like the map of Columbus's day, while the evolutionists glory in the truth of present day pictures taken from outer space. All scientists believed in the crude map of the earth as they thought it existed 500 years ago. All scientists now believe in the modern picture of the earth taken from space. This is typical of true, but completely irrelevant information, frequently supplied by evolutionists.

This comparison has nothing to do with supporting macroevolution and like many of the examples presented, simply has no relevance. If the writers were trying to prove macroevolution why would they even present these pictures?

Early in the 1984 booklet the following was written on page 6:

> "Religion and science are separate and mutually exclusive realms of Human thought whose presentation in the same context leads to misunderstanding, both of scientific theory, and religious beliefs."

Again, this is an atheistic statement that has nothing to do with proving macroevolution. The book goes on to say "The theory of evolution has successfully withstood the tests of science many, many times." This is typical of the many claims that are true only for microevolution and therefore completely misleading when not clearly identified. There has been no test or proof of macroevolution which is the only area contested.

Another statement in the booklet on page 7:

> "The hypothesis of special creation has, over nearly two centuries been repeatedly and sympathetically considered and rejected on evidential grounds by qualified observers and experimentalists. In the forms given in the first two chapters of Genesis, it is now an invalidated hypothesis."

What atheistic rubbish. The scientists have determined through evidence and experiments that Genesis is wrong. This is an absurd statement and has nothing to do with trying to prove macroevolution. It is the utmost arrogance for a scientist to say they can scientifically prove that creation never occurred thousands of years ago. While trying to prove creation did not occur, where is the evidence that life started from nothing, in some prehistoric pond?

Another illustration in the book on page 9, depicts the celestial system when it was believed the earth was the center of our solar system. Many years ago all scientists thought the earth was the center of our solar system. In later years Galileo proved that the sun is the center of our solar system. All scientists now obviously believe this. This is another irrelevant issue, attempting to mislead, while having nothing to do with either creation or evolution. It merely is an attempt to show that an old belief has been changed and associate creation with it by being old, while evolution is claimed to be the new science. How does this attempt to prove macroevolution?

The book claims creation is impossible because it "reverses the scientific process." This is merely another atheist comment that has no relevance in any attempt to prove macroevolution. This is also meaningless since creation is not the issue and this is not evidence to support macroevolution. It is not possible to prove that creation did not occur. Evolutionists have the responsibility to prove macroevolution, which they cannot do and therefore continue with irrelevant comments.

The Grand Canyon, on page 15, is shown as an example of different strata of rocks that accumulated during the succession of geological ages. The Grand Canyon is clear evidence against the uniformitarian concept, since nothing is happening today, or has occurred in all of recorded history, that would explain the formation of the canyon. But what does this have to do with the evolutionists requirement to prove macroevolution?

The 1984 booklet goes into detail to try to show that similarities prove a common ancestor. The arm of a man, fin of a whale, leg of a dog and wing of a bat have somewhat similar bone structures. The evolutionists claim that they must have therefore had the same ancestors. The Christian belief is, that is the way God created them. Where is the proof or evidence that they had a common ancestor? There is none. A simple explanation is that God created them that way. Any evidence that could be true for creation by God as well as by some kind of macroevolution is no evidence at all.

If there were an argument about whether I took a bus or a taxi to work, and I said I'm here, so that proves I took a taxi. This would be ridiculous since it doesn't disprove the alternative. Evolutionists frequently use similar examples by showing evidence that would be true for either belief, and claim it supports evolution. Stephen Jay Gould used similar false logic when he said, "We know evolution is true because we are here."

The 1984 NAS book states:

> "Thus molecular biology validates the already impressive evidence that all living organisms from bacteria to humans, are ultimately descended from common ancestors."

This is totally false. There is no evidence that similarity in DNA, or any other detail, could reveal a common ancestor between humans and animals. The book goes on to state, "The missing links that troubled Darwin and his followers are no longer missing." Again, this is a totally false statement. If anything there are fewer so called missing links today and none have been proven. Why do you think they are still called missing links and are never identified? In their search for missing links evolutionists concentrate on old fossils where they know their claims can't be proven wrong. They know there are no macroevolution changes since the beginning of recorded history. Old fossils that can't be proven are all they have.

The 1984 booklet also believes in the theory of biogenesis, the belief that all life came from existing life, while at the same time believe in the spontaneous generation of life that started from non-life, in a prehistoric pond millions of years ago. Can you say hypocrite? Again, no evidence for macroevolution.

The book's conclusion, on page 26, stated: "No body of beliefs that has its origin in doctrinal material rather than scientific observation should be admitted as science..." Again the search for truth has been preempted by an atheist concept that permits no truth if it questions Darwinian evolution.

The 1984 booklet makes it clear that it is atheist dominated. No real evidence to prove macroevolution is provided. If a good definition of brainwashing would be to permit only the teaching of one side of an issue, teach that side in a biased or fraudulent manner, and completely deny any evidence to the contrary, then our public schools are unquestioningly brainwashing our students on evolution.

But in spite of the complete dominance by the atheistic, "scientific" community over our society, the average American was still skeptical. Fourteen years later, after the first booklet on creation, in 1998 the NAS published their second book titled, "Teaching About Evolution and the Nature of Science". In the preface, the following quote, made it clear the evolutionists were not wining the hearts of the people:

> "Fewer than one-half of American adults believe that humans evolved from earlier species. More than one-half of Americans say they would like to have creationism taught in the public school classrooms."

This 1998 publication by the National Academy of Sciences is another unscientific and biased attack against the Christian belief in creation, and a support for atheistic evolution. The errors in this book are also too numerous to give it a complete review here. Only some of those erroneous or fraudulent examples, that are not repetitious from the first booklet will be mentioned. At the start it should be mentioned that nowhere in the 140 pages will you be able to find the words microevolution or macroevolution. Shortly after its publication I contacted the agency and questioned, in writing, why the words were not used or discussed in the book. The eventual answer was that they simply chose not to. I don't blame them for the omission. If I were trying to support a completely indefensible position, I certainly would not bring up something that would destroy my entire argument.

One of the many errors in the book is the claim throughout the book that evolution is supported by an "enormous body of evidence." Many other statements are made that are true only for microevolution but the implication is that they are referring to evolution in general. This is completely false.

The following quotes from the book are examples where the book refers only to evolution, but are true only for microevolution and false for macroevolution:

"...the most important concept in modern biology, a concept essential to understanding key aspects of living things-biological evolution

"...the enormous body of data supporting evolution and because of the importance of evolution as a central concept in understanding our planet"

"The document you are about to read summarizes the overwhelming observational evidence for evolution.".

"Chapter 1...provides scientific definitions of several common terms..."

(Note: microevolution and macroevolution definitions are conveniently missing.)

"...there is no evidence that evolution has not occurred."

"...concepts such as evolution that are supported by overwhelming evidence."

"When a theory is supported by as much evidence as evolution, it is held with a very high degree of confidence."

"In this sense, evolution is one of the strongest and most useful scientific theories we have."

"Teaching biology without evolution would be like teaching Civics and never mentioning the United States Constitution."

"…evolution has been tested and has a lot of evidence to support it."

"…evidence that demonstrate beyond any reasonable doubt that evolution occurred as a historical process and continues today."

"Evolution in natural communities arises from both constraints and opportunities."

These are only some of the statements in the book that refer only to evolution when in fact they are unquestionable true only for microevolution. In most cases they are completely false or unsubstantiated for macroevolution. It is obvious why the evolutionists do not want to clearly identify micro and macroevolution. It would eliminate nearly all of their evidence.

There are many other misleading or highly questionable comments. One statement is "Our knowledge of fossil intermediates is actually pretty good". This implies a clear knowledge of many missing links, which is completely false. This is typical of many evolutionist statements that say their beliefs have been proven many times over, and we don't need any more proof, when in fact, they have no proof at all.

In order to prove the ancient ages of fossils, evolutionists use various methods, all of which involve estimates, assumptions and probabilities. One of the methods used is circular reasoning. Since rocks can't be dated directly, the fossils are dated and then the rocks are dated from the fossils. Then wherever similar rocks are located, those new fossils are dated from the rocks.

A factory watchman had the job of blowing the six o'clock whistle every day at the factory. To be sure he had the correct time, he went by the local jewelers store early every morning to set his watch by the big clock in the window. One morning when he went by the store to set his watch, the owner was there. He told the owner he was setting his watch by the clock in the window. The owner said "yes, that clock is accurate. I set it by the 6 o'clock whistle at the factory every day." So much for circular reasoning.

The NAS book also supports the long discredited concept of embryos going through the development stages of the species they descended from.

In addition, the book also contains a lot of general information that has no bearing on evolution because it could be equally true for creation. None of it specifically shows evidence for macroevolution. Irrelevant information is presented as if it supports evolution such as natural selection. Of course natural selection is true. It merely allows for the individuals best suited to the environment to survive. It can create no new genetic information and is part of microevolution. The book also covers other general information such as explaining logic and a few other concepts that are really irrelevant to the issue. There is no real evidence to support macroevolution other than some gratuitous claims or statements.

On November 27, 2007, a creation-evolution debate was held at the Dothan Opera House, between creationist Dr. Robert Carter and evolutionist, Mr. Rick Pierson. One of the main points made to support evolution, was the existence of multiple pseudo genes in both humans and chimps. These similar, non functioning genes, are claimed to be evidence of descent from a common species. While it is claimed these genes don't do anything. It is equally plausible that science has not yet been able to determine what they do.

About 150 years ago, science had declared there were over 100 vestigial organs in the human body. These included the appendix, tonsils, thyroid and others. It was claimed these, so called, vestigial organs served no known purpose and therefore must have been left over from the earlier species from which we evolved. But since that time, a specific purpose has been determined for nearly all the miss-named vestigial organs. Similarly, in the case of pseudo genes, it would seem more likely that science simply has not yet determined the purpose of those genes. This is certainly no proof of macroevolution.

In all of the arguments, or evidence, presented by evolutionists, not one can prove macroevolution. All of their arguments are based on the assumption that macroevolution is true and therefore, if it is true, such and such would exist. Examples are the similarities of the limbs of man and some animals, some similarity in the DNA of man and apes, etc. etc. But all of the examples given by evolutionists could also be true for creation. So the examples are meaningless. But it is true that by natural means, life cannot come from non-life. Matter cannot create intelligence and one species cannot create new genetic information to form a more advanced species

CHAPTER SEVEN

A GODLY NATION, ADRIFT

This great nation of ours was clearly founded as a Christian nation. Those that deny it are either ignorant of this nation's history or they have an agenda which they put ahead of reality. The Christian God is referred to in nearly all of the early documents leading to the foundation of this nation. One of the earliest, the Mayflower Compact, on Nov. 11th 1620, started out with:

> "In the name of God, amen,..."and then "having undertaken, for the glory of God and the advancement of the Christian faith and honor of our King and country, a voyage to plant the first colony in the Northern part of Virginia, do by these presents solemnly and mutually in the presence of God..."

Starting with the Mayflower Compact above, and down through 300 years, this nation was clearly recognized as a Christian nation. There are numerous historical books that show this as an absolute fact. David Barton in "Our Godly Heritage," and other books by him, are excellent for the skeptic. Catherine Millard, a French born lady who later became so proud of becoming an American citizen and a born again Christian, that she did considerable research and published "God's Signature Over the Nation's Capital."

Catherine Millard's book is impressive with all the direct references to God in our nation's capital. Ms Millard lists far too many examples to include here. If anyone, seriously and honestly, doubts the Christian background of this nation, please get Catherine Millard's or David Barton's books. It is not possible for an intelligent person to read either of these books and still deny God's handiwork in our nation's background. An example I will mention here is on the highest point in the nation's capital. On the aluminum cap atop the Washington monument, are inscribed the words, "Laus Deo" which is to say, "Praise be to God."

Since the aluminum cap on top of the Washington monument is not viewable, the National Park Service (NPS) created a plaque to be on display near the base that explained the fact and purpose of the aluminum cap. And of course it ended with the phrase "Laus Deo." In 2007, the NPS, in following the government's attempt to remove God from our capital whenever possible, replaced this plaque with another. The new plaque, omitted the final words "Laus Deo", in fact, the only words that actually were on the top aluminum cap.

Also, "The American Covenant, the Untold Story" by Foster and Swanson, published by the Mayflower Institute, discloses the real, early America. The book, "The Christian History of the Constitution of the United States of America" by the Foundation for American Christian Education, stated:

> "The highest glory of the American revolution was this: it connected in one indissoluble bond, the principles of civil government with the principles of Christianity."

After many years of research and study, both in America and overseas, in 1828, Noah Webster published his first "American Dictionary of the English Language." In the preface to the book he wrote:

> "The United States commenced their existence under circumstances wholly novel and unexampled in the history of nations. They commenced with civilization, with learning, with science, with constitutions of free government, and with that best gift of God to man, the Christian religion."

These, and many other books and documents, clearly establish a nation founded on the principles of the Christian religion. If anyone, having read this far, still does not believe this nation was founded as a Christian nation, then he is without hope, and should pick up his pointed hat, and go sit in the corner.

After I had written most of this, a new book came out by Peter Lillback, titled "Wall of Misconception." In nearly 200 pages, Mr. Lillback covers the miss-named wall of separation, in great detail. Anyone sitting in the corner, if he can read this book, and if he is still not convinced this is a Godly nation, he should turn in his dunce cap and report to the nearest asylum.

This book assumes, and accepts the Christian belief that there is one God, and the Bible is God's word, without error. The Bible is quite clear that not one jot or title is to be changed. Those Christian churches that claim they take their Bible seriously, but not literally, are in error. Those churches that place their own church-run hierarchy above the Bible are also in error. If some readers disagree with the views herein, their argument is not with me, but with the Bible.

If the Bible is true, then the belief in Darwinian evolution must be the biggest fraud ever perpetrated on mankind. In fact, if it is a fraud, it should not be too difficult to expose. The question is often proposed, which should take precedence, science or the Bible? God is supreme and His word is without error. The most important area where this may be questioned, is in Genesis. The Bible is clear that God created everything in six days. Present day secularists deny the six day creation, in part, by using an atheist definition of science. They will only accept something as true if it meets their definition of science, which denies a God. Others will fall into the pit of denying God's word since they have listened to the naysayers and look for ways to compromise God with science. Chapter 8 on theistic evolution discusses some of these compromises.

Our nation today is faced with many problems. Are we facing these problems with a Godly Christian attitude or are we embracing most of the evils? When being tempted, Jesus said "get thee behind me Satan." Are we as a nation, now saying the opposite, "get thee behind me Jesus?" After all, morality does inhibit all our evil thoughts and actions. Sinful actions generally yield short term pleasure. The drunkard is usually happy and enjoying himself, until the next morning. We rationalize many of our evils by redefining evil, or by covering the evil with a veil that makes the evil sound good. We refer to abortion as pro-choice knowing everyone favors a freedom to choose. We ignore the fact that the choice is to kill an unborn baby. After all we are a free nation. Aren't we? Little attention is paid to the killing of nearly 50 million babies in the womb, under the words pro-choice. Anyone who thinks God is being fooled, raise your hand.

As recently as January 18, 2008, the mayor of Fredericksburg Virginia, was quoted in an editorial in the Fredericksburg Free Lance-Star as saying:

> "Upwards of half the children being born at Mary Washington Hospital are out-of-wedlock births. We have a higher than average teen pregnancy rate."

I suppose we should be thankful for the births rather than abortions, but is there anyone that cannot recognize a morality problem here?

While this is not meant to be a political book, one cannot discuss American life, moral issues and the evils of evolution, and ignore the moral differences between the two major political parties. That would be to ignore the elephant in the corner. Recently a congressional aide was explaining our political system to some foreigners and he said, "We have two major political parties in our country, the evil party and the stupid party. I am proud to say I am a member of the stupid party." He is of course, referring to the Republican party as the stupid party, and I could present considerable evidence to support that. He is obviously referring to the Democratic party as the evil party. There is no doubt that the Democratic party is the party of abortion, and so evil seems to be a good fit. I recently asked a Democratic politician whether it was fair to refer to the Democratic party as evil, because of abortion, and he replied that he didn't always vote pro-abortion. But facts are facts, and the Democratic party is almost unanimous in voting pro-abortion, even to the extent of supporting partial birth abortion.

Those favoring abortion use deceitful methods while supporting their position. The word "pro-choice", by itself, is meaningless. What if I asked the question, "why is a horse?" It is equally meaningless unless I clarify the meaning. The word pro-choice is used by itself to mask the real meaning which is pro-choice to kill an unborn child. In an attempt to cover up the immorality of such a position the pro-abortion crowd might say, "I would not have an abortion myself, but who am I to put my morality on someone else?" Would that kind of argument make sense if I said, "I would not to own a slave, but who am I to put my morality on someone else?" Another frequent comment is, we are trying to make abortion safe and rare. If there is nothing wrong with abortion, why are they trying to make it rare? The hypocritical stand on this issue by those calling themselves pro-choice, is obvious.

The Democratic party is also the party of evolution and denies any attempt to support creation. I do not know why the creation-evolution controversy should be a political one, except that our political parties are apparently based on perpetual conflict. The result is that when one party takes a stand on an issue, the other side automatically takes the other side. Unfortunately then, it seems, when one party takes a patriotic stand, the other side must end up with an opposite view.

I believe it is accurate to say President Bush, based on some of his actions, is destroying the Republican party. I also believe that comments coming from the far left-wing, mostly in the Democratic party, are so obsessed with hating President Bush that their actions are tending to destroy the nation. Whether we should be in the present conflict in Iraq or not, the fact is, we are in a war where Americans are dying. Comments coming from the far left are nearly the same as the propaganda from the enemy. In any other war that would have been considered treasonous.

Prior to our entry into World War II, a large majority of Americans believed in the America First organization and did not want us to get into the war. The day after the Japanese attack at Pearl Harbor the America First organization completely disbanded. It was obvious to all Americans then, that whether we should be in the war or not was no longer an issue. We were in the war and everyone united behind the war effort. Unfortunately today, Americans are not united, and many, for political purposes, are still arguing that we should not be in the war.

An example of how we have lost our Christian anchor was recently brought to my attention, when a Christian lady said some of her Republican friends were considering voting for a Democratic candidate. When I informed her, that he was a member of the abortion party, she said, "Oh they don't care about that." Abortion, the killing of nearly 50 million babies in the womb, is something many people don't even care about anymore.

Since evil is running rampant in our society, we tend to over react. We have completely discarded common sense, logic and God. We have established some "zero tolerance" concepts in our laws that have resulted in treating all apparent violations the same. A small child taking a plastic knife to school in his lunch is just as guilty as someone taking a switch blade. Or a six-year-old boy that playfully kisses a young girl on the cheek is considered a sex offender. Just recently a seven year old boy was suspended from school for a day, for making a drawing of two stick men, one of them pointing a stick pistol at the other. The boy labeled "me" on one, and another boy's name on the other. He said they were playing with water guns.

I would not have survived as a child in today's society. When I was a child we actually made guns that would shoot large rubber bands. We would make our own bullets out of old inner tubes that would obviously be illegal today, and cut them into large rubber bands. We played war and to my knowledge no one was ever hurt. I only tell this now because I believe the statute of limitations has expired on assault with a rubber band gun. My wife, who was raised in a different part of the country, claims she was once the victim of one of these rubber band guns, so I guess it was a nation-wide crime spree.

A recent case involving the alleged rape of an exotic dancer (read prostitute), by three men during a party at a Duke University frat house resulted in national attention to a prosecutor run amok. After almost a year of being vilified by the press, the University, and most of the local community, the men were all exonerated. The deceitful actions of the District Attorney involved, who had evidence from the start the men were innocent, resulted in his disbarment. If only this were an isolated case.

A recent case in July 2007 involved two 7th grade boys who ran down the school hall playfully slapping several girls on the butt as they ran by. The two were hauled off to jail, not permitted to see their parents for 24 hours, kept in jail for five days, taken to court in shackles and prison garb and charged with a felony sex offense. The only real criminal here is the over-reacting District Attorney. These are only two examples of a legal system gone astray because we have lost touch with basic Christian moral values. The prosecutors have lost sight of their purpose, which should be to seek justice, but have turned the law into a perverted crutch to further their own careers.

Many of the absurdities in our society are encouraged and exacerbated by our judicial system. In 1966, the Supreme Court ruled in the now famous Miranda case, that anyone charged with an offense had to be given a warning as to what his constitutional rights were before he could be questioned. Any information obtained before the Miranda warning was given, no matter how condemning, would be inadmissible. While the constitution does state no one can be compelled to testify against himself, it does not state a suspect must be given a warning, in advance, as to what his rights are. Needless to say, admitted killers can now go free if they can show they gave incriminating evidence before they were read their rights.

Some known criminals have taken advantage of this by intentionally admitting to a crime before they are given the Miranda warning, and then later claiming the admission, and all information obtained from it, is inadmissible. If properly used by a criminal, the Miranda is a get out of jail free card. In some cases it seems, the criminals are smarter than the justices. Maybe "smarter than" is not the best phrase to use. How about, "less stupid."

As a side issue, in justifying the Miranda decision, the court referred to the judicial systems of India, Ceylon and Scotland. One might question, where on earth did the court read in the Constitution they have sworn to uphold, the authority to use foreign governments actions, beliefs, or customs in their rulings? While I have not checked other rulings to see how far this concept of Supreme Court rulings being based on what some other foreign countries have done, it is being brought up more and more.

In 1947 the Supreme Court decision in Everson v. Board of Education erected a wall of separation between church and state. In a series of later rulings, all kinds of Christian expressions in the public area were banned.

We have the best legal system in the world. We have a terrible legal system. Both statements are probably true. Activist judges that claim to follow the law and take an oath to uphold the Constitution, do their best to change the law and the Constitution, to what they believe it should be. A strong case can be made to show our legal system, especially our activist courts, led by the Supreme Court, have taken the lead in destroying us as a Christian nation.

One of the worst decisions of the Court was in the Dred Scott case where the Court determined that slaves were merely property and had no rights. The possible harm of that decision was short lived since the civil war that followed, as well as the 13th amendment, made the decision moot.

The nation was not so lucky on other decisions. In the infamous Roe vs Wade case in 1972, the court outdid itself in using logic more attuned to an idiot than to judges. The Texas law that was involved, claimed that "life begins at conception." When the male sperm and the female egg combine, that is the start of a new human life. Nothing more is necessary, or even added, other than food for sustenance, and shelter. The Supreme Court denied this and kept referring to "potential life", and stated:

> "We need not resolve the difficult question of when life begins. When those trained in the respective disciplines of medicine, philosophy, and theology, are unable to arrive at any consensus, the judiciary, at this point in the development of man's knowledge, is not in a position to speculate as to the answer."

The logic and concept behind this is somewhere between idiotic and stupid. It is ridiculous for them to say they can challenge a scientific fact by saying philosophers and theologians don't agree. Why Americans, for the most part, remained calm after such a blatant, blasphemous, and anti-Christian ruling, is hard to understand. The result of the Roe vs Wade ruling is about 50 million babies killed in the womb, and still counting. Is God watching?

Alexander Hamilton, in the Federalist Papers No. 78 wrote:

> "Whoever attentively considers the different departments of power must perceive that, in a government in which they are separated from each other, the judiciary, from the nature of its functions, will always be the least dangerous to the political rights of the Constitution; because it will be least in a capacity to annoy or injure them."… "It proves incontestably that the judiciary is beyond comparison, the weakest of the three departments of power."

While this was the opinion of Alexander Hamilton in 1787, it was probably based on his assumption that we would have honest and upright judges that, being free from politics, would rule in accordance with the law. However, by 1821, Thomas Jefferson's views were completely different and more prophetic. He wrote:

> "It has long been my opinion and I have never shrunk from its expression...that the germ of dissolution of our federal government is in the constitution of the federal judiciary; an irresponsible body – for impeachment is scarcely a scarecrow – working like gravity by night and by day, gaining a little today and a little tomorrow, and advancing its noiseless step like a thief, over the field of jurisdiction, until all shall be usurped from the states, and the government of all be consolidated into one. To this I am opposed; because, when all government, domestic and foreign, in little as in great things, shall be drawn to Washington as the center of all power, it will render powerless the checks provided of one government on another, and will become as venal and oppressive as the government from which we separated."

History has shown who was right. Hamilton's views were based on having justices with integrity. He did not allow for the corruption of almost unlimited power delegated to the Supreme Court justices who arrogantly put their own views on what they believed the Constitution should say, over what it actually says. This has resulted in the judicial tyranny we have today. Words like "living Constitution" and "penumbras and emanations" as well as considering what other godless nations are doing have separated our nation's laws from what the true Constitution had established.

The Supreme Court has involved the federal government in what should be state authorized areas in stretching logic, for example, by ruling, in one case, that an elevator operator in a building comes under interstate trade.

The court's rulings are just as obvious and no less despicable than the wicked witch in the land of Oz who claimed, "words mean anything I want them to mean."

Our founding fathers established a constitution that they believed would survive for all time. In fact, realizing that times might change and changes might be necessary, they allowed for specific procedures to change the constitution. Our Supreme Court Justices were to be given life-time tenure with the belief that it would remove them from politics. Unfortunately that turned out to be a mistake. While the justices were removed from partisan politics, they were not removed from their own personal politics and arrogance. The old saying that "power corrupts and absolute power corrupts absolutely", is proven by the record of the Supreme Court. Instead of the Justices using their life time tenure as a reason to be above politics, they have instead used it to set themselves up as arrogant gods, in a super legislature, uncontrolled by the people.

The Court is supposed to rule as to whether laws passed by the legislature are constitutional. The Court's deviation from this is almost unbelievable. In the Roe v Wade case the Court justified their disastrous ruling by referring to "penumbras and emanations" of the Constitution. Using this shading of the facts, the Court went on to deny human life, as if it were in the Constitution.

If the court claimed, as they did, that they were not sure when life began, then logic would dictate, if not sure, play it safe and assume it might be life. Can you imagine someone demolishing a building and saying "I'm not sure if anyone was inside, so I blew it up."

In her book, "Power to the People," Laura Ingraham, popular syndicated radio show host and author, discussed the fact that every January tens of thousands of Americans come from all over the United States on Roe's anniversary to march and protest the Supreme Court's abortion stand. Ms. Ingraham asks the obvious question, "Why is a public rally aimed at a court? Aren't the courts supposed to operate outside of politics?" If the Court ruled properly, as it should, then any protests should be to the legislature to change the law. It is clearly understood, but not admitted by either side, that it is the Supreme Court that is illegally making the law, not the legislature. We have tacitly accepted the unelected Justices of the Supreme Court as a super legislature and this is by definition, judicial tyranny. I am sure that in their wildest dreams, our founding fathers never anticipated our Supreme Court would stray so far that they would put their own personal interpretation into the constitution and simply change it as they saw fit. Except for Thomas Jefferson, whose comments in the Federalist Papers seemed to predict exactly what would happen. Our nation was founded as a Christian nation and the founding fathers had every right to expect that all our elected leaders, and appointed officials, would be men of integrity. How wrong they were.

When our Constitution was written, the writers were intent on preventing any one denomination from imposing its views on the self governing individual through the power of civil government. The following statement by the eminent professor and theologian, Charles Hodge, Princeton Seminary, in 1876, illustrates the thinking that once prevailed concerning our nation and its purpose:

> "The proposition that the United States of America are a Christian and Protestant nation, is not so much the assertion of a principle as the statement of fact. That fact is not simply that the great majority of the people are Christians and Protestants, but that the organic life, the institutions, laws, and official action of the government, whether that action be legislative, judicial, or executive, is and of right should be, and in fact must be, in accordance with the principles of protestant Christianity."

There are also numerous books and older Supreme Court rulings that are consistent with the fact that we were once a Christian nation. However, in 1961, in the Torasco vs Watkins case, the Supreme Court recognized secular humanism as a religion. In delivering the unanimous decision, Justice Hugo Black stated:

> "Among religions in this country which do not teach what would generally be considered a belief in the existence of God are Buddhism, Taoism, Ethical Culture, Secular Humanism, and others."

So if the Court has ruled that Secular Humanism is a religion, and evolution is the basic belief of Secular Humanism, why do courts consistently rule out creation because it supports a religion, while evolution is acceptable because it is science? Can you say hypocrite?

We have become so passive that almost anything done by our bureaucratic leaders, at any level, is accepted. We are operating under the new golden rule: "He who has the gold, makes the rules." If the Supreme Court should rule that the sun rises in the west, don't argue, just change all the maps.

There is a rumor, started by someone in Australia, (the down under state) that explorers in Antarctica recently uncovered a giant sign at the South Pole that said "THIS END UP." It was quickly covered up again, but not before an Australian saw it, so the rumor goes. For heavens sake, don't tell the Supreme Court.

As bad as the Roe v Wade ruling was and still is, some previous rulings that threw the Bible out of the schools and claimed a wall of separation between church and state, may have done more damage to this once Christian nation. A personal letter written by Thomas Jefferson was the source of the Supreme Court's ruling on the wall of separation between church and state. Mr. Jefferson's personal letter had no official standing to change or clarify the Constitution in any way. Thomas Jefferson was not at the convention that wrote the Constitution. It borders on the fantasy that the Supreme Court would take this letter as justification for a total change in our nation's life style and moral values.

Several disastrous Supreme Court decisions in 1962 and 1963 openly repudiated the transcendent Biblical natural law standards which had prevailed. In David Barton's book, "Original Intent, The Courts, The Constitution and Religion" the author stated that in the thirty years, from 1963 to 1993, birth rates for unwed girls, aged 15 to 19 had quadrupled. Violent offenses in the nation rose by 600%. Cases of the sexual disease, Gonorrhea, rose by 400%, educational achievement, as revealed by SAT scores, dropped from 970 to 900. The female heads of households, which indicates the break down of Christian family life, rose by two and one half times. Mr. Barton clearly showed that the sudden disastrous change in our moral standards was directly due to the Supreme Court rulings. Thank you, Supreme Court.

The widespread acceptance of extreme homosexual lifestyles has been primarily responsible for the world-wide AIDS epidemic. Untold millions are being spent on trying to find a cure, while nothing is really being done to address the real cause, which is immoral promiscuity. During World War Two, the military was concerned with two or three sexually transmitted diseases. Now there are more than twenty and they are becoming prevalent in our middle schools.

Our Universities have for the most part, established co-ed dorms where various degrees of immoral co-habitation are permitted. A recent book by Tom Wolfe, "I am Charlotte Simmons," reveals almost unimaginable obscenities at a premier university. Although fiction, the book is the result of the author's considerable research at several large universities, and the immoralities he writes about have been more than verified by other sources.

An Associated Press report in June, 1970, claimed that sexual violence among youth is on the increase. Some psychologists blame the 40% increase, over two decades, on a society saturated with sex and violence. On a different but related subject, on more than one occasion a few young men and women have been detained voluntarily, in a zoo-like atmosphere, to see how they would react. They were just trying to get in a touch with their ancestors.

In November, 1980, the Supreme Court ruled the Ten Commandments could not be posted on the wall of a school room in Kentucky because seeing the words of the Mosaic law on the wall, may induce children to read, meditate upon, perhaps to venerate, and obey the commandments. Can anything be more idiotic than this decision against the Ten Commandments?

Why has this once proud Christian nation degenerated to such an extent? I know some individuals who are very strongly opposed to abortion and have almost dedicated their life to this effort. There are some organizations formed solely to oppose the openly aggressive, homosexual lifestyle. Some organizations attempt to control the daily smut we receive on our TV every day. While all these efforts that oppose the various immoral practices are to be commended, we need to recognize there is a single underlying cause to all these problems. If the ship is sinking because of a series of small holes, you don't go looking for a bucket, you plug the holes.

We should be concentrating more on attacking and discrediting the godless Darwinian evolution belief, and many of the other problems will be more easily handled. If we stop teaching kids they are nothing more than advanced animals, they will stop acting like animals. If we teach fixed moral values, then teen-agers will stop believing everyone can establish their own set of beliefs.

A few years ago a twelve year old girl wrote for advice from "Abby." She said many of her friends had tried Marijuana and she didn't think it was a problem, so should she try it? Abby's response was, "find out as much as you can about it and then do what you think is right for you." This is an incredibly stupid answer, by Christian standards, and it should be by anyone's standards. There are some Christian organizations that are really promoting anti-Christian efforts by accepting the so called wall of separation, and believe we should allow religion only in the church. Listening to the local evening news today, is more like listening to a police report.

A major split is occurring in the world-wide Episcopal Church, as well as others, over the issue of homosexuals. Should men be allowed to marry men? Should active homosexuals be allowed to become priests? No intelligent person in his right mind, can truthfully say that the Bible does not condemn homosexual practice. It is an abomination. The words in the Bible are clear. They are not my words, but God's. While I do not have an issue with two men living together in sin, their problem will be with God. But I do object to the active, in-your-face, obscene homosexuals that want to publicize their actions through parades, forcing their life style on young children through the Man Boy Love Association, and putting in the public schools information that homosexuality is an acceptable life style. It is not. It is an abomination, according to the Bible, and a deadly life style. Practicing homosexual persons will not likely, on average, live into their 50's, losing anywhere from 30 % to 40% of the life span expected in Western society – well into the 70s.

While any efforts that attempt to address the evils in our land, are commendable, none of them address the basic cause, or even attempt to determine the basic cause. Darwinian evolution, denies God, and I believe is the underlying cause of most of the immorality and depravity we see in our society today. Evolution permits all kinds of sexual perversion, establishes the concept that "if it feels good, do it," denies any fixed moral values but teaches only moral relativity, and has convinced most Americans that we are nothing more than a higher form of our animal ancestors. How can kids who are taught they are only animals, be expected not to act like animals?

One author refuted evolution as the cause of teen pregnancy, teen drugs, teen age rapes and teen age violence. He claimed evolution can't be blamed, because teenagers do not suddenly develop rebellious mentalities as the result of studying the theory of evolution. Students who typically pursue such acts are not always the most studious, and therefore probably did not retain much of what they studied about the theory. This would seem to be an unbelievably simple-minded comment. Of course evolution is not the direct cause of these problems. The real problem is that evolutionary theory permeates our society – it can be seen in our TV programs, in the movies forced on us from Hollywood, in nearly all our public school books, in all our major universities, in nearly all PBS documentaries, in all our local and state school boards, in all our local and federal courts and worst of all, in many of our Christian churches. It teaches we are no better than animals, and in fact are really advanced animals. It is this undermining of our entire moral structure that leads to all the problems. Has our present society degenerated to the same corrupt status as the Biblical condition stated in Judges 17:6 "…every man did that which was right in his own eyes?"

Can there be any doubt that when Darwinian evolution is finally recognized as the fraud that it is, that there is a God that created all things, that there is an afterlife where we will all some day be held accountable, then our society will change?

Some of our legislatures have passed hate crime laws. To expand these laws to cover homosexuals is a clear effort by the homosexual lobby in order to silence any dissent. Hate crime laws are being supported and directed by anti-Christians in order to silent or suppress Christian opposition to sodomy. Why do we need a hate crime law? If some one is assaulted or murdered, we might suspect the guilty party had no love for the victim. The guilty should be punished according to the physical crime committed. Should we get into the mind of the perpetrator and determine whether he hated the person he had beaten up? Should it matter what he was thinking at the time, or merely what was physically done? An article by John W. Whitehead, president of the Rutherford Institute, appeared in the Fredericksburg Free Lance-Star on Oct. 17, 2007. Mr. Whitehead stated:

"Unfortunately, more and more Americans – in their effort to censor, silence, or sanitize what they find offensive - have resorted to banning certain words and criminalizing the thoughts behind certain actions. However, attempts to curtail the actions and speech of a few individuals are now threatening the constitutional rights of all Americans."

"Such is the danger posed by the Matthew Shepard Act, which was named after a gay college student who was savagely beaten to death in Wyoming in 1998, This act would expand the 1969 federal hate crime law to include crimes motivated by a person's actual or perceived sexual orientation, gender, identity, or disability."

Those guilty of the Shepard murder have already been tried and been sentenced to death or life in prison. A hate crime bill would add nothing to the case it is named after. If you think such a law cannot harm innocent Americans, think again. Canada already has such a law and a pastor was recently arrested and charged with a hate crime for reading out of his Bible in church. While he was exonerated, this time, how about the next time?

CHAPTER EIGHT

THEISTIC EVOLUTION

It had been stated earlier that there are two mutually exclusive world views of the origins of mankind and the universe. A Christian view that God created everything and the evolutionist's belief that everything just happened by natural causes. But this premise is not accepted by everyone. As in any complicated and controversial issue, there are always those who, for one reason or another, try to find a middle ground.

Theistic evolutionists do not accept the premise of two world views. They object to being associated with atheists. While it is true that all atheists are evolutionists, it is not true that all evolutionists are atheists. At no time should theistic evolutionists be referred to as atheists. However, they do support issues that are dogmatically defended by atheists. Theistic evolutionists refute the plain and simple straight forward reading of the Bible that has been accepted for centuries, and in accepting some middle ground, are in fact accepting some of the atheist's beliefs.

Theistic evolutionists do not accept the Bible as the clear word of God, but believe the Bible must be compared to science, to determine whether its passages are true. But once one starts down the slope of questioning the Bible, where does it end? There are many specific miracles clearly stated in the Bible. They all defy science. If they didn't, they wouldn't be miracles. So when anyone starts questioning God's word because it doesn't agree with science, when did they depart from their faith in God? If God could not have created everything in six days as clearly stated, what other miracles in the Bible are denied? It would seem logical to me that a Christian should accept all the miracles in the Bible, or none. It almost sounds like believing in God on Sunday but not the rest of the week.

William Jennings Bryan, three times presidential candidate, former Secretary of State, famous Christian apologist and probably best known for his role as the prosecutor in the Scopes monkey trial in 1925, had made some interesting comments on theistic evolution. In one of his presentations over eighty years ago, he stated he would make no difference between theistic evolution and atheistic evolution. He stated:

> "...the theistic evolutionist and the atheistic evolutionists walk hand in hand until they reach the beginning of life. They are nearer together than either one of them is to the Christian and they think more of each other than they do of the Christian. They travel back to the beginning of life. When they get there they politely separate; The theistic evolutionist affectionately bids his companion goodbye and says, at this point I must assume the existence of God."

Mr. Bryan goes on to say the atheist is not doing much harm, because when a man denies the existence of God, he puts himself beyond the pale of reason. He stated:

> "The man I am afraid of is the theistic evolutionist who says he believes in God but leads the student who trusts him, and follows him back, step by step, until God is out of sight."

Mr. Bryan also wrote:

> "I regard theistic evolution as simply an anesthetic which deadens the pain while atheism removes the religion. No preacher can stand behind the pulpit and deny the existence of a God; but some stand behind the pulpit and preach things that cannot be true if the Bible is true."

What were Satan's first words in the Bible? The Serpent said to Eve, "Has God indeed said you shall not eat of every tree of the garden?"

First, God's word is questioned, then denied. The serpent then said "You will not surely die." Is this different from those who, today, question God's word on creation? Did God really say "In the beginning...?" And how many Christians say it wasn't really the beginning. Did God really say all was created in six days? Today many Christians say he didn't really mean six days, or the six days weren't really normal days. Or maybe there were a few millions of years between the days, or maybe the universe was in existence for millions of years before the six days started. Is Satan merely taking another approach in causing us to doubt God's word?

Ken Ham, from Answers in Genesis, had an interesting comment on the different interpretations of the meaning of the word "day." I have paraphrased it but he said essentially, "In my father's day, it took three days to drive across the country, driving only by day." The word day is used three times, each in a different context, yet each is perfectly clear. From the context it is clear that the first day is a period of time, the second day refers to a full 24 hour day, and the third refers to only the daylight period of a day. It is obvious that the word day, can have different meanings. It is equally obvious that the exact meaning is easily determined by the context in which it is used. The six days of creation in Genesis could not be clearer. They are, without a doubt, meant to be normal, 24-hour days. Almost everyone is familiar with the term RINO, meaning a Republican in Name Only. Someone who claims to be a republican but does not really support basic republican values. I am using a new term here, in a similar vein. It is CINO, a Christian in Name Only. One who claims to be a Christian but does not always support Christian Biblical values.

Those believing in some form of theistic evolution are not evil or anti-Christian. But then neither did Adam or Eve have evil intentions when they believed the serpent. What if God's word on creation is clear, plain and simple and means exactly what it says and was so understood for centuries? What was it that started the theistic evolutionists questioning of the clear words of the Bible? It was the alleged scientific evidence that purported to disagree with the Genesis account of creation.

For the last 300 years or so, scientists have presented evidence that purports to show that the earth is very old, at least millions of years old. Fossils seemed to indicate a slow progression of life from the simple species to the more complex. Many Christians were unable to challenge the science presented, but were not willing to abandon God. The result was a compromise by re-interpreting some Bible versus to make the Bible compatible with science. The initial error of the compromisers was first of all, they lost their faith that the Bible is God's word, without error. And second, that science never really proved any of its claims. All of the so called scientific facts were really based on many assumptions that may not be true, along with interpretations that were slanted to support evolution.

Our present world is dominated by those seeking compromise of almost anything controversial. It seems that the general response to conflicting views is that the truth must be somewhere in the middle. A few books are written that purport to show that, with proper interpretation, science and the Bible can be compromised to everyone's satisfaction. The main thesis of Stephen Jay Gould's book "Rocks of Ages" is, what he refers to as NOMA, Non-Overlapping Magesteria. Those are high priced words meaning we can all get along if we don't overlap our areas of belief. His compromise, that Christians keep their beliefs in the churches, since they are religious, and evolutionists will keep their beliefs in the secular community since they represent real science. A better word for all of the evolution compromises is surrender.

Any effort to compromise is doomed from the start. Atheists are not interested in even admitting the possibility of a God, and Christians will never accept a compromise that eliminates God. When the devil took Jesus to the mountain top and showed him all the kingdoms of the world and their glory, he said "All these things I will give you if you will fall down and worship me." Jesus did not say "can't we compromise and just all get along?" No. Jesus said "Away with you Satan, for it is written, you shall worship the Lord your God, and only him shall you serve."

To a Christian that believes the Bible is God's word, there is no interest in compromising on anything that God has said. In the beginning means exactly that. Nothing existed before the beginning but God. Some authors would have us believe that one would really need a Doctors degree in several advanced scientific fields, in order to understand what "In the beginning" really means.

Why would alleged new scientific findings, starting many decades ago, change any Christian's belief in the miracle of the six day creation? It would seem that most Christians' belief in God remained strong, but they were not willing to challenge the alleged science. They were willing to acknowledge that maybe a little bit of the Bible could be re-interpreted. They searched the Bible for other passages they would also need to re-interpret, to lend support to this new meaning. These Christians had opened Pandora's Box, and several theistic evolution theories were born. Some of them will be discussed here.

This concept of believing science has proven the Bible inaccurate, may have had some credibility seventy-five or a hundred years ago. Our society was then first being assaulted with evidence of the ancient age of the earth, the long distance to the stars, the fossils, etc…In the face of this scientific evidence, few Christians could stand up and say "This is God's word and it is without error."

Many Christians were not aware that historic science was not necessarily true, but was based on assumptions by generally biased individuals. We will see in later chapters that the latest scientific evidence does more to support creation than evolution, and that much of the earlier accepted scientific evidence that supported evolution, has turned out to be based only on false assumptions and inferences.

There are several different forms of theistic evolution and all, without exception, are based on alleged scientific evidence that tends to deny God's miracles. Adam was created as an adult on the sixth day. "Oh no" cried some theistic evolutionists. "God could not have created Adam with an apparent age allowing for years that didn't exist." But that is exactly what God did. The stars were created for light at night. "Oh no" claim some theistic evolutionists, who admit God could have created the stars, but not the light from them.

There was an Irishman who preferred the moon to the sun, because the sun shines in the day-time when there is no need of it, while the moon shines in the night time. There is a rumor that the Irishman was an honorary member of the National Academy of Sciences, but this is unverified. In our court system if the jury hears particularly damaging evidence the judge doesn't want the jury to hear, he merely tells the jury, "ignore the evidence you just heard." Similarly, since I don't want to be accused of spreading a rumor, please disregard this paragraph.

All of the theistic evolutionists are well meaning and truly seek to find a middle ground between the Bible's account of creation and the scientists who deny it. But nowhere in the Bible does it say we should seek a compromise. In Matthew 10:34, Jesus said "Think not that I am come to send peace on earth: I came not to send peace, but a sword." Does this sound like God wants us to seek a compromise between his word and science? I don't think so.

Science has never proven any of the Bible wrong. Would you not think a Bible believing Christian would say the Bible is God's word, it is without error, and that any difference between the Bible and science would necessarily be one of God's miracles, an error in the reported science, or a misinterpretation of the Bible. A classic case of misinterpretation of the Bible is the Catholic reluctance for many years to accept the fact that the earth revolves around the sun.

For centuries, the ancient Aristotle theory of geocentrism, that the earth was the center of our solar system and the sun revolved around the earth, was accepted by all scientists. In the 17th century, Galileo proved that the earth revolved around the sun. The Catholic Church and its scientific advisers denied this. The Church claimed it violated the Bible in such areas as where God caused the sun to stand still. If God stopped the sun, then it must have been moving. Of course this was merely a misinterpretation of the Bible. We still refer to the sun as rising in the east, while we know it is only a relative movement, and it is really the earth that is moving. (at least until our Supreme Court rules otherwise)

Some issues between the Bible and science are not easily resolved and belief in theistic evolution is one of these. Theistic evolution takes several forms, such as the Gap theory, the Day Age theory, and Progressive Creation, and each with its scientific supporters. All of these theistic evolutionist's beliefs started by doubting the Bible's account of the six day creation.

In responding to the clear words in the Bible that states that the earth and all its living forms were created in six days, Hugh Ross, author of "The Fingerprint of God", and founder of "Reasons to Believe" stated:

> "Because of the implausibility of such a position, many reject the Bible out of hand, without seriously investigating its message or even reading for themselves the relevant passages."

But why is it implausible to accept the miracle of creation as clearly stated in Genesis? Do Mr. Ross and others who deny God's creation, also believe all God's miracles are implausible? How about the truth of Moses parting the Red Sea, or the virgin birth, or the resurrection from the dead, to name a few? If we accept an all powerful God, how can any miracle be implausible? Mr. Ross, and his scientific knowledge of the cosmos, has led him to deny God's input if it disagrees with his scientific knowledge. But those that deny God's miracles sometimes resort to silly comments. In referring to creation with an apparent age, Mr. Ross said:

> "Taken to its logical conclusion, the appearance of age theory would imply that we could not establish that our past experience actually occurred. For example we could have been created just a few hours ago with the creator implanting memory, material possessions, scars and hardening of the arteries, to make us appear and feel older than we are."

Of course the answer to this childish response is that God created everything in six days, and nothing has been created since that time. The argument is a silly "straw man" response, bringing up something ridiculous in an attempt to discredit God's obvious creation with an apparent age.

As mentioned earlier, all theistic evolutionists attempt to re-interpret many Bible verses to fit whatever they think science has proven. Hugh Ross bases his logic on at least two assumptions. The first is that God could not have created anything with an apparent age. The second is based on scientific evidence the stars are all moving apart and the beginning of time would be identified by backing them all up in time until they all arrived at a common point, which would be at the Big Bang.

The first, involving the appearance of age, has already been discredited. The second, leading back to the Big Bang, is not logical, nor does it have any possibility of ever being able to be proven. Based on the red shift of the light from the stars, there does appear to be some solid evidence the universe is expanding. If so, it would be logical to assume all the stars were closer together in the past. So backing them up in time is a legitimate exercise. The error is in assuming they would have all started from a single point and they would have reached that point about fifteen billion years ago. This is an atheist series of assumptions and is not supported by facts. If the stars are all moving apart, then back them up to where they were when God created them, a little over six thousand years ago. Makes sense to me.

Neither scenario above can ever be proven. One would expect a Christian to believe the creation by God a little over six thousand years ago, since the Bible is fairly clear on this. Atheists must believe in the rather far fetched belief that the entire universe was at one time in a single point of zero dimensions. Now that takes real faith. Mr. Ross claims this single point is called a singularity because it only happened that one time in history, and he claimed "A singularity is not a point, but the whole of three dimensional space, compressed to zero size." So all the matter in the universe, at one time, occupied zero space, but had infinite density. A new math equation has been discovered. Zero size, times infinite density, equals the universe

In his search to challenge the clear words of the Bible, for something on which to base his version of theistic evolution, Chuck Missler doesn't waste any time. He claims the first three words in the Bible, "In the beginning," are wrong. Mr. Missler claims that was not really the beginning and re-interprets a few Bible passages to support his views. Why? Because Mr. Missler is unwilling to accept God's miracle of creation. He also claims God could not have created Adam with an apparent age, because that would be a lie, and God can't lie. Can one possibly visualize how Adam could have been created, without an apparent age?

Mr. Missler also equates the decaying of the velocity of light as having something to do with a day of creation being a long period of time. Hugh Ross, a fellow theistic evangelist, claims the so called proof of the decaying of the speed of light is ludicrous. Why not just accept the Bible as God's word? Occum's Razor says, "All things being equal, you should choose the simplest over the complex."

Gorman Gray in his book, "The Age of the Universe: What are the Biblical Limits," takes a different approach to the creation issue. He claims all the stars and the universe were created an unspecified billions of years ago. But the earth was kept in the dark and barren until Genesis 1, when

God started his six day creation of the earth's biosphere. Apparently this will satisfy the scientist's arguments of the long age of the universe and the Biblical account of a six day creation.

Mr. Gray's thesis is based on his training in Biblical and ancient languages, which led to his re-interpretation of Genesis. The forward to his book, a glowing support for this thesis, was written by a language expert, Mr. David E. Eckman, PhD, Associate Professor of Hebrew at Western Seminary, San Jose, California.

I am certainly not qualified to discuss the intricacies of the Hebrew language or the various translations involved. One might question, however, whether there were not Hebrew scholars somewhere in the past three or four thousand years that were equally qualified in translation, that never came up with this unusual thesis.

Mr. Gray discredits the mandatory young earth interpretation of Genesis. He claims that:

> "for creationists to demand that scientists believe galaxies must be less than 10,000 years old is an inexcusable offense to the scientific community."

Big deal. Scientists are offended at all of God's miracles. Should we deny all of God's miracles so the atheist scientists won't be offended? Mr. Gray also stated:

> "God has preserved the integrity of his word by establishing first of all a literal factual document. Behind the primary, literal meaning, he has hidden secondary meanings."

Apparently Mr. Gray is the only one that has access, or even knows about these hidden meanings in the Bible. While part of the Bible contains parables, as Jesus made clear, to open the plain interpretation of the Bible to hidden secondary meaning would be to destroy the Bible as God's word. (Incidentally, that is exactly what is destroying our

Constitution, when so called penumbras and emanations are involved by some court judges in changing the clear wording, to a totally different meaning.)

According to Mr. Gray: "The correct interpretation of scripture will fit comfortably with a correct view of science..." He also stated:

> "We must be willing to adjust our thinking about Exodus 20:11, (which states) For in six days the Lord made the heavens and the earth, the sea and all that is in them, and rested the seventh day. Therefore the Lord blessed the Sabbath day and hallowed it".

Of course it is not possible to fit the Bible comfortably within secular science unless one is willing to forego all of God's miracles. To do so would not be a compromise but a complete surrender of the Christian faith. Did God direct the writing of the Bible in a manner that we would have to wait for over 6,000 years after the creation, for our intellectual PhD's to explain to us commoners, what God really meant.? In the beginning, was not really the beginning, and a day was not really a day? Jesus said: "Assuredly I say unto you, unless you are converted and become as little children, you will by no means enter the kingdom of heaven" This is almost the opposite of some of the theistic evolutionists that claim we must have a few advanced degrees in several subjects in order to understand the Bible.

It had been reported over 75 years ago, that approximately 40% of freshmen lost their faith in college. More recently, a comment in the July 25, 2002 periodical by Focus on the Family quoted a Southern Baptist Council as saying 88% of children raised in evangelical homes leave the church at the age of 18, never to return. Whatever the percentages are, it is obvious our Christian youth are losing their faith when they leave home, or go off to college. And why wouldn't they?

Consider the effects of growing up in a typical Christian church, either protestant, Baptist or Catholic, where theistic evolution is taught, and all your friends and close acquaintances believe the same thing. Then you leave home, and the rest of the world, especially if you go to college, teaches atheism. Darwinian evolution is taught as a fact in all your classes, and believed by all your new friends. How can you defend your faith when they correctly point out you don't even believe the Bible yourself? How can it be the word of God when the first verses are wrong? You have never been taught about Jesus as the creator, but only about Jesus on the cross.

The real damage is done to the Christian youth that are never given a solid Christian background based on the inerrancy of the Bible and the six day creation. When these youth leave home for college or to spend more time with their peers, they are easy prey for atheist evolutionists. All, or most, of their new friends, and all of their teachers, will present evolution as a fact. Creationists are depicted as ignorant hillbillies. How can a young Christian defend the Bible as God's word when he has been taught the first few verses in Genesis are not true? They are told by their teachers and friends that science has proven the Bible wrong. How can you believe in a loving God with all the suffering and cruelty in the world? How can you deny all the scientific proof of the fossils, an earth that has to be billions of years old? Even your own pastor admits the Bible contains errors. How can an intelligent person deny science? Unfortunately, many Christian youth can't defend Christianity, and therefore, say goodbye to God. In the previous mentioned court cases that challenged Darwinian evolution in the schools, it seems incredible, but several alleged Christians went hand in hand with the atheists, that opposed teaching Intelligent Design.

For many Christians, ignoring a belief in the six day creation, is not a problem. Older citizens can live with the erroneous belief that denies creation, accept some kind of compromise, and live their lives as good Christians. They live in a Christian community, associate mostly with Christians, and in general ignore whether God created everything in six days or fifteen billion years. To them, the question of what's the difference what we believe about creation, may make sense. They are the feel-good Christians, or the Sunday or holiday only Christians. They associate only, for the most part, with other Christians. But when their children leave this sheltered environment and go off to college, they are thrust in a different, atheist dominated world. The damage to the youth is enormous. Without a real foundation based on the inerrancy of the Bible and the six day creation, many lose their faith.

The story of Charles Templeton fits well into this chapter on theistic evolution. Not because he believed in theistic evolution, but because Charles Templeton's story reveals how even a widely accepted Christian evangelist had failed, because he never had the basic Christian faith to believe in the Genesis account of creation.

Mr. Templeton, a native of Canada, met Billy Graham in 1945 when they were both in their twenties. They became close friends and for quite some time Templeton would alternate with Billy Graham in the pulpit. Templeton spoke nightly to stadium crowds of up to 30,000 people. It was obvious they were the two most effective exponents of mass evangelism in North America.

But Mr. Templeton was facing a growing dilemma. In his later book "Farewell to God" he stated," I was beginning to question some of the essentials of the Christian faith." and "I had always doubted the Genesis account of creation..." Lacking any formal theological training and with only a ninth grade education, he applied to and was accepted, at Princeton. Following his completion of theological studies there, he was hired for "preaching missions" by the National Council of Churches (NCC). There is little doubt that Princeton, the NCC, and the Presbyterian Church where he later worked, all reinforced his doubts about creation and other Bible stories.

Nineteen years after he left Toronto, he abandoned the Christian faith and returned. He claimed he was an agnostic, but his beliefs seem to clearly identify him as an atheist. Whatever he called himself, he became an outspoken anti-Christian. Most of Mr. Templeton's book, "Farewell to God" consisted of one condemnation of the Bible after another. He stated that:

> "We were told that God created the world in six days and rested on the seventh. But every physicist in the world will tell you that such a view is nonsense; that it took billions of years for the universe, our galaxy, our solar system and our world to evolve to its present..."

In questioning every miracle of creation, Mr. Templeton stated:

> "Whom should you believe, the theologians or the physicists...the theologians or the geneticists...the theologians or the geologists? ...whom should you believe, the Christian church or your own common sense?"

All the miracles of creation are denied by modern day scientists; which shouldn't surprise anyone. If they weren't denied by scientists, they wouldn't be miracles. The bottom line to all Mr. Templeton's doubts were that God's miracles couldn't be true because science had proven them impossible. How many Christians today are having their faith tested because they have been told, or taught in school, that science has proven God's miracles could not have happened.

Mr. Templeton goes on to question nearly every major miracle in the Bible, including the creation, Noah and the flood, Moses and the Ten Commandments, the virgin birth, and the resurrection. He goes on to say evolution is proven by Australopithecus, Lucy, and the ape to man belief as if they were all proven facts.

Unfortunately Charles Templeton's fall from grace may be fairly common. It seems, however, that he never really had the faith since from the start he questioned the word of God in the creation account. It is the same question facing theistic evolutionists today. How can you believe the Bible is the word of God when you don't believe the first few verses? If you doubt the beginning, you are likely to start questioning other parts and then look to science to support them. Apparently no one could give Mr. Templeton the answers that others can now get from this book, or numerous other sources now available.

In all of Mr. Templeton's rejection of the Bible, nothing he came up with was factual. There was no smoking gun, while present day science is providing a smoking gun against Darwinian evolution.

There have been other evangelists in the past, and probably some today, that have the ability to convince crowds, through their own personality, of whatever they are selling. The shallowness of some of the believers is evident when, if the evangelist commits some sinful act, the followers then forsake God. Real faith is centered on God and is unaffected by the actions of any mortals.

The question frequently comes up in many churches, why make a big deal out of it? What's the difference as long as we all believe in God? The difference is enormous. Doubting the six day creation challenges the very credibility of the Bible. Why do you think that research by the Southern Baptist Council on Family Life reported the disturbing fact that eighty percent of the children, raised in evangelical homes, leave the church by the age of eighteen, never to return? Why is this nation, founded on Christian principles, now a post Christian if not an anti-Christian nation?

How can you expect children, or anyone, to believe the Bible is God's word if you deny the first, most important part, on creation? We permit our secular government schools to teach evolution as a fact and no contrary information is even allowed. We not only deny any Christian teaching in our schools, but we permit teaching about other fringe religions, whether it be Indian folk lore, situation ethics, Satanism or moral anarchy. Everyone, even children, are taught to decide for themselves, what is right and wrong.

A book by Jonathan Sarfati, "Refuting Compromise", is an excellent and very detailed refutation of "Progressive Creationism", as popularized by Hugh Ross in his Reasons to Believe ministry. While Hugh Ross has very specific beliefs, not shared by all theistic evolutionists, any Christian that questions a six day creation should find this book convincing.

The difference between believing the Bible is God's word as written or believing a distorted compromise version, may determine whether this nation will survive as a nation under God. Before we can win this great battle against evolution, our churches must recognize there is a battle. Many are reluctant to do so.

How simple and logical it would be to simply accept the Bible on faith, know it is always correct, and recognize that all current scientific facts fit very well in the Bible, if one also accepts God's miracles. It is only the false interpretations, assumptions, and refusal to accept God's ancient miracles that create doubt.

There is a Western song that says "Happiness is Lubbock, Texas in the rear view mirror." If you will pardon the analogy, I would like to say, for Christians and for patriotic Americans, "Happiness, is Darwinian evolution in history's rear view mirror."

CHAPTER NINE

LEGISLATION AND THE COURTS

For many years the evolutionists have tried to establish false rules in the creation vs evolution debate. They have consistently claimed that creation is religion while evolution is science. The courts have determined that anything religious (read Christian) must be banned from our public schools. You know; wall of separation and all that.

In many creation-evolution debates, the evolutionists have frequently spent much of their time trying to discredit creation, solely because it is religion, while claiming evolution is science. Unfortunately many creationists try to counter this by showing that creation is also science. It is not. The proper argument, and the only one that makes sense, is that neither creation, nor the evolutionist's belief of the start of life, is science. Both are beliefs of what might have happened at least thousands of years ago. As such, neither can be proven but we can find evidence today that will tend to support or deny one belief or the other.

In several court cases the creationists have tried to show that creation is not religion, but is also science. Of course this is not only false, it is also a losing argument. Stop to think for a minute. Can anyone in his right mind deny that creation is a religious belief? Of course not. The truth is that both creation and evolution are religious beliefs.

Evolution is the belief of secular humanism which has already been declared a religion by the Supreme Court. If we can't teach creation in the public schools because it is religion, then the same should apply to evolution.

The scientific opposition to creation, if it is legitimate and honest, would be to show how life started, according to the secular humanists. Is it science to believe life started in some pre-historic pond, or in some ocean's depths, all by itself, with no intelligent input, and therefore matter created intelligence?

More recently, evidence of ancient happenings has been referred to as historic science. Historic science can't be proven because it cannot be tested or repeated. Obviously the credibility of historic science depends primarily, if not completely, on the scientists that are making the interpretations, evaluations or assumptions. Historic science would always be considered a belief that may or may not be true.

In the 1920's there were several states that made the teaching of evolution, that man descended from the lower animals, illegal. It was the reflection of our Christian heritage, reacting to the introduction of evolution on the national scene. After the Scopes trial in 1925, evolution and atheism became socially acceptable. Doubts were created in the minds of many Christians about the inerrancy of the Bible, and especially concerning the account of creation. Even William Jennings Bryan, the prosecutor at the Scopes trial, and as solid a Christian as you could find, succumbed to the evolutionists tirade and was beginning to question a six day creation.

Following the Scopes trial, no attempt was made to deny teaching evolution in the public schools. Secular evolution gradually took over due to the aggressive nature of the evolutionists, the atheist dominated ACLU, the media and the school system. By their own documents, the National Academy of Sciences changed their definition of science from one in 1976 that included a search for truth to one in 1984 that denied truth if it supported creation in any way. This attempt to put creation in a box and remove it from the public schools, while glorifying Darwin as the new god, was very successful. At least as far back as sixty years ago, encyclopedias and biology books have considered Darwinian evolution a fact.

Several attempts have been made in recent years to get some of the evidence supporting creation, back into the schools. In 1987 a Louisiana law was overturned by the

Supreme Court that would have required equal treatment of creation and evolution. The court did not rule against teaching creation in the schools, it ruled against making it a requirement. The court claimed the purpose of the law was to advance religion. Apparently the Court doesn't read their own rulings or they would know they had previously ruled that secular humanism is a religion and evolution is the belief of secular humanism. Hypocrites or ignorance?

Other courts have similarly rejected any attempts to legislate the teaching of creation. And even though the Supreme Court did not deny the teaching of creation, leaving it up to the teachers, what the Court had allowed was denied by local school boards and principals. Several cases are documented to show individual teachers have been banned from teaching any aspect of creation, or from even questioning Darwinian evolution. The courts and the public schools are not what one would consider friendly to Christians.

I have a video where Eugenie Scott, Executive Director, National Center for Science Education, stated essentially that she didn't oppose teaching any evidence against evolution, if any existed, but she didn't know of any. I'm sure Ms. Scott is a very intelligent woman. She has been totally indoctrinated into the evolution belief, but her education and knowledge of the evidence that supports creation and denies evolution is lacking. Any educated person, knowledgeable in a controversial subject, would know all the arguments both for and against his belief. Ms. Scott's lack of knowledge that there is considerable evidence against Darwinian evolution indicates indoctrination.

Occasionally a school board, at the state or local level, will attempt to change their standards, to at least permit the questioning of the Darwinian belief. of evolution. When this happens, it usually gets nation wide attention. The ACLU, People for the American Way, Americans United for Separation of Church and State, and other atheist dominated groups, all pile on to beat back the Christians. Incredibly, even some Christian theistic evolutionists, join the opposition under the false belief that they must support the wall of separation, but are in fact, favoring indoctrination over education.

While school boards all across the country are occasionally faced with this conflict, the Kansas school board case is a good example. Through a series of events and local conflicts the Kansas state school board succeeded in rewriting the science standards that did little beyond questioning Darwinian evolution. In a protest of this action, the Governor, numerous state legislators, and the presidents of six state universities in Kansas, issued a public condemnation of the Board's action. At the next election the local school board was voted out of office and the requirements changed. Had this not been changed it would have gone to the court system where courts are incredibly anti-Christian. This debate will continue until common sense and a more enlightened community exists. People must be made aware that Darwinian evolution is the basic belief of secular humanism, which is a religion according to the Supreme Court. Also the effort should be made to compare Darwinian evolution to the truth. Is there any evidence to prove it? If we are even going to mention creation it should be only in comparison with the evolutionist's beginning of life in some small pond, or wherever.

Recently Creationists have tried to use the Intelligent Design (ID) movement to challenge Darwinian evolution. Christians on the Dover Pennsylvania School Board tried, unsuccessfully, to use the ID concept to challenge evolution. This resulted in the federal court case, Kitzmiller vs Dover Area School District, in 2005. The Christians lost, and the case resulted in the decree by Judge John Jones III, that banned any teaching of ID, since it violated the separation of church and state.

The defendants foolishly tried to show that ID was not religious, and was not associated with creation. Their own documents proved to be part of their defeat, when it was shown that their ID argument had clearly evolved from creation. It also didn't help any when two of the school board members had been caught lying under oath. Instead of the widely publicized federal court case that was lost, how simple and effective it would have been, if the Christians had opted for a voluntary insert in the biology books, placed only by students. More on the necessity for voluntary efforts in Chapter ten.

Our judicial system's anti-Christian bias and incredible arrogance has taken it far beyond merely ruling against creation. Do you believe Americans, especially Christians, charged with any criminal offense have a right to a fair jury trial? Think again. The right to a fair jury trial is slipping away.

In 17th century England a law was passed intending to require all citizens to worship only in the Anglican Church. A youthful William Penn, being a Quaker, disagreed with the law. Unable to attend his church which had been padlocked, and blocked by armed dragoons, he attempted to preach in the street. On Sunday, August 14, 1670, William Penn was arrested and confined in Newgate Prison, awaiting trial.

The judicial custom at that time, was to detain any nearby citizen and make them jurors in a jury trial. Edward D. Bushell was one of the citizens detained and forced to be on the jury. It was also customary for the court justices to order a finding of guilty. The jury would leave for the jury room, and return a few minutes later with a finding of guilty. Led by Edward Bushell, the jurors refused to find Penn guilty. The jurors were threatened, fined, and in some cases tortured for defying the court.

To make a long story short, the jury was eventually exonerated through an appeal that clearly established, once and for all, the right of a jury to rule on the law as well as the facts of a case. The judge cannot order the jury to find the defendant guilty. This case is covered in detail in the book "The Ordeal of Edward Bushell" by Godfrey D. Lehman. This trial clearly established the basic underlying principle of a jury's right to rule on both the facts and the law of the case, and has been a bedrock foundation in American law since the nation was founded. Webster's first "American

Dictionary of the English Language" published in 1828, defined jury in part as, "...consisting usually of twelve men, attend courts to try matters of fact in civil causes, and to determine both the law and the fact in criminal prosecutions."

The Supreme Court has upheld this on many occasions. In U.S. vs Spock 1969, the court stated:

> "Put simply, the right to be tried by a jury of ones peers finally extracted from the King would be meaningless if the King's judges could call the turn...Bushell's case...In the exercise of its functions, not only must the jury be free from direct control in its verdict, but it must be free from judicial pressure..."

Also in U.S. vs Moylan 1969, the court stated:

> "The jury has the undisputed power to acquit even if Its verdict is contrary to the law as given by the judge and contrary to the evidence."

And in U.S. vs Wilson 1980 the court stated:

> "In criminal cases jury is entitled to acquit Defendant because it has no sympathy for the government's position: it has general veto power..."

So it is completely clear that a jury has the right to rule on both the law and the facts of the case. That was clearly established in English law in 1670. It was carried over, from the beginning, into American law, was clearly defined in Webster's first American dictionary, and has been upheld by our Supreme Court on many occasions. One might think it is settled law. But, if you think so, you have underestimated the arrogance of our judges.

A booklet, prepared for jurors in the Circuit Courts of the Commonwealth by the Judicial Council of Virginia is given to all prospective jurors. The booklet, titled "The Answer Book for Jury Service," contains the following, "You (the jurors) decide the questions of facts. After you have decided the questions of fact, you will apply the law to the facts as directed by the judge at the end of the trial." Also, under jury instructions, "The jurors must accept and follow the law as instructed by the judge even though they may have a different idea about what the law is or ought to be."

It is clear that the courts in Virginia, deny to the defendant, a jury that has been notified of the jury's right to rule on both the law and the facts of the case. Even this is compounded by giving the jury final instructions that claim, if the jurors find certain facts to be true, then they must find the defendant guilty. The judicial arrogance is obvious since the Supreme Court has made it perfectly clear that, no matter what the evidence shows, a judge can never direct a jury to come up with a guilty verdict.

Denying the defendant the opportunity to present all of his evidence, in defense or mitigation, is another example of judicial tyranny. In a trial I was involved with several years ago, concerning the peaceful blocking of the door to an abortion clinic, the court approved the prosecution's Motion in Limine, (before the trial started) that denied the defendant from using the Necessity Defense. Necessity is the defense that claims the charged offense was necessary in order to avoid a worse action. The classic example of this is someone violating a no trespassing area in order to save a child drowning in a swimming pool. To be convicted of trespassing, without the jury even being aware of the attempt to save a drowning child, would obviously deny justice.

But that isn't all. In misdemeanor criminal cases in Virginia, the jury sets the punishment at the same time they decide the verdict. So what about possible extenuating circumstances? Sorry. They can't be brought up at the initial trial, and after the jury decision- too late.

In any jury trial the judge totally controls what can be said and what evidence can be presented to the jury. While judges frequently give lip service to the concept that the jury system is the best way to determine facts, they then undercut this by limiting the facts that can be presented to the jury. For example, judges will let all evidence be presented if the judge is hearing the case, but if a jury is hearing the case much of the evidence might be excluded. On one case I am familiar with, the judge told the defendants they could present all their evidence if they would not seek a jury trial, but he would deny part of their evidence if they insisted on a jury trial. The jury might be influenced in a way the judge did not like, so they would be denied certain evidence.

In addition to the Motions in Limine, how about the frequent so called side bars, where the attorneys and the judge conspire over whether certain information can be given to the jury? But the jury is supposed to give an intelligent and just determination of the facts, when it is obvious that some information is withheld from them. In some cases the judge will tell a defendant that he cannot use a certain defense, or the court may deny the defendant from using certain words, even though they may be the crux of the defense. (I can attest to both since I was the defendant)

In one case of a peaceful blocking of an abortion clinic, the judge told the defendant (with the jury absent) "You will not use the words potential life, abortion is murder or necessity defense" Lots of luck with what's left of your defense.

Many prosecutors are more determined in seeking a conviction, than in finding justice. With the introduction of DNA evidence, dozens of convicted men have later been found innocent. Some of them were on death row. Many of these false convictions were obtained by evidence being withheld from the defense and the jury. But it also works both ways. There are cases where an obviously guilty man is freed because evidence proving his guilt was denied to the jury.

There are many examples of a court system run amok. One recent example concerned a man that sued a cleaner for 50 million dollars for losing or ruining his suit.

Why the judge didn't throw this out immediately defies common sense. Another well known case involved the twinkie defense. I think the defendant pleaded insanity from eating too many twinkies. Insanity could have been better ascribed to the judge for letting the case proceed. Or the case of a woman who sued McDonald's restaurant when she spilled a hot cup of coffee in her lap while driving off.

In Texas, an Edwards County Deputy Sheriff, recently completed serving one year in prison for shooting at the tires of a fleeing van he had previously stopped. The driver, hauling illegal aliens, drove off and tried to run over the Deputy. The prosecutor claimed deadly force is not allowed to stop a fleeing car. I'm sure that if the jury were aware of the rights of a jury to rule on the law as well as the facts, the Deputy would not have been convicted.

You want to hear something even more absurd? At the time of this writing the Supreme Court has agreed to hear a convicted murderer's appeal that execution by lethal injection is cruel and unusual punishment. Good grief. Giving an injection first that deadens all pain and feelings, and then two more that finally results in death is probably the most painless way to execute anyone. Since our Supreme Court can't really believe something so absurd, it is obvious they have an agenda. They had previously stopped all executions and it appears the no death penalty crowd has influenced the court and they may find some penumbras and emanations in the Constitution that would make all executions illegal.

There seems to be little doubt that our judicial system has lost its anchor to a once Christian base where justice was the goal, and has evolved into an arrogant and tyrannical force of legalism, that is destroying our constitutional republic. Most of the above is unknown or ignored by most citizens. It will not be easily corrected and then only after real Christians wake up, and our nation returns to a nation under God.

In the meantime, and certainly in the foreseeable future, it would be a complete waste of time to bring any court case concerning creation or evolution to the attention of the courts. All challenges to the establishment's bias against creation, and its current recognition of evolution being a fact, must be made on a voluntary basis. No legislation, or even directives to promote creation, or even question evolution, will be successful. Seeking directives from school boards will not be successful, and in some cases in the past, such actions have had repercussions in getting Christian members defeated at the next election. Positive results will only be achieved through voluntary efforts. Some of these are suggested in the final chapter.

CHAPTER TEN

WHAT CAN WE DO?

I would not be a true Christian if I didn't admit that prayer should be our first, and necessary, step. I also would not be a realist if I didn't recognize that for many Christians, that might be their only step. Prayer is not enough. Our nation and the world is in serious trouble. Our once Christian nation, founded as all Christians believe, basking in the glory of the Lord, has turned it's back on God. Our first action is to recognize that we are in a war with the satanic forces of evil. Darwinian evolution is dead and the corpse is beginning to smell. It might take another generation to bury the body since most of the older generation, raised on the alleged fact of evolution, will never admit they have lived and believed in such a colossal lie. For the most part they will prefer to go to their grave, believing in the lie, rather than admit they were wrong.

Younger generations must be taught the truth, be willing to consider the faith of the one and only God of creation, and look with an unbiased eye on the false evidence of evolution. They will clearly see the major difference between microevolution and macroevolution. A return of this nation to its Godly roots is not only possible, it is absolutely necessary, if this nation is to survive. While I have so far quoted very little from the Bible, I would like to quote from 2nd Chronicles 7:14,

"If my people, which are called by my name, shall humble themselves, and pray, and seek my face, and turn from their wicked ways; then will I hear from heaven, and will forgive their sin, and will heal their land."

Obviously the first step is prayer, but nobody ever accomplished anything with one step. We must recognize and confront the evil facing us and recognize the underlying cause of most of the evils in our nation today is Darwinian evolution. We can fight this evil with truth, through our youth and younger generations. Wherever evolution is taught it should be questioned and challenged. Every Christian youth should be taught that Christian belief is based solidly on the six day creation and the inerrancy of the Bible. It has been a disaster to teach only the Jesus of the Cross and the New Testament, while at the same time denying the Biblical account of God at the creation. If we don't get the major Christian churches to return to the inerrancy of the Bible, and actively teach the creation account, I do not believe this nation will survive.

You won't see a sign outside an abortion clinic that says "Open by approval of your local church." But that is the truth. That must be changed. A sign in front of a Christian church once said, "We take the Bible seriously, but not literally." That must also be changed.

The politically correct concept that we must recognize all religions as equal, is wrong. We must return to a Christian nation based on Christian ideals and Christian moral values. There is nothing wrong with believing Christianity is the one true religion based on the one and only God of the Universe. If you don't believe that, you are not a Christian. Some years ago bumper stickers were seen that said "God is dead". My answer is that "my God is alive, sorry about yours."

While this is a Christian nation, it has always recognized the right of any citizen to believe whatever he wishes. Freedom of religion is not just an empty phrase. In a capitalistic and Christian nation, citizens have the right to be wrong. They can believe in any god they wish, or none. However, they do not have the right to have their beliefs, whatever they are, affect our nation's laws or customs. They cannot force their views or beliefs into our public schools or government or society. The Supreme Court must return to rulings that recognize the Constitution as supreme over their individual biases and that this is a Christian nation.

The ACLU, People For the American Way, and other anti-Christian organizations must be de-funded, voluntarily, by educating the public. Should we allow other religions to build their churches, mosques, or whatever? Of course. But other religions beliefs and customs should not be allowed in our public schools. Our public schools should be Christian based, reflecting a Christian nation, with the Bible welcomed, prayer as each state or community determines and the ten commandments posted wherever local governments desire. The courts should butt out and return to their legitimate purpose of ruling on the existing law, not writing new law. Is all this possible? Yes, but only if we return to the God of the Bible, our mainline Christian churches develop a back bone, and their members cease being CINO's (Christians in name only).

In the past, several state legislatures or school boards, have attempted to legally attach a disclaimer in the public school biology textbooks. The disclaimer usually was only a mild questioning of evolution or a statement that creation should be considered. No matter what the disclaimer, or how insignificant the challenge to evolution, it brought the atheists out in force. As one evolutionist said, "We can't even allow a divine foot in the door." The anti-Christian organizations such as the ACLU, Americans for the Separation of Church and State, and others, bring out their big guns in challenging any such effort in the courts. Christians don't have a chance in our present, anti-Christian court system.

Recognizing that we now live in an anti-Christian society, that includes the courts, the news media, and sad to say, some of our religious institutions, any attempt to bring forth the truth of a Christian God and to challenge macro evolution must be done on a voluntary basis.

To return this nation to its Christian roots will require an epic undertaking. It may not even be possible, but we must assume it is, and work for eventual success. First of all, we must recognize that we are in a war involving good and evil. We must recognize that atheist evolutionists are destroying this nation, morally first, and then politically. We must change the minds of the majority of the population to accept the fact that the Christian belief in creation will be politically correct. We can not achieve success in the courts or in the legislatures, with their existing atheistic leanings. The lead must come from the Christian churches in America, but they must first return to a belief in the God of creation as well as Jesus on the cross.

For the kids, home schooling is one option. But it is not available to everyone. Some parents rationalize sending their kids to public school on the assumption they would be a good influence on the other kids. Get real. Would you put sheep in with wolves to teach them to be non-aggressive? If children are to be a good influence on others in school they must first be educated on the creation belief. The kids must be taught by parents who believe and attend churches that believe. We should try to reach kids as early, as at least fifth grade. There is a TV program showing 5th graders are pretty smart. And their minds are still pliable enough that they can be miss-lead into believing the truth.

What are some of the things kids can do now in our public schools? First, they must be educated on the basic facts in this book and the many other books supporting creation and Christian moral values that explain the real truth about evolution. They can politely question everything that comes up concerning evolution. Students could prepare a disclaimer to put in their biology book that would question evolution. This disclaimer could question why the book doesn't give examples of macroevolution, why the book lists examples of microevolution when trying to support macroevolution. The disclaimer might question how the evolutionists explain life starting when they admit all life comes from existing life. These disclaimers would have to be made up by the students, carried voluntarily, offered to other students, and also provide a copy to the instructor. The key to the success of this would be the basic knowledge of the Christian students and the fact that it is voluntary. You may be surprised at the willingness, of some teachers and many students, to listen to legitimate discussions of the issue.

By asking proper questions in class, such as, "all examples given for evolution are merely microevolution, where are examples of macroevolution?" Or, "how can science explain life starting from nothing, when matter cannot create intelligence?" "Why are many examples given to support evolution that could also be true for creation?" "Why is evolution's explanation of events millions of years ago considered facts, when nothing that happened before recorded history can be proven?" "How can uniformitarianism be true when nothing that happened in all of recorded history can explain the Grand Canyon or marine fossils on top of all mountains?" Other questions can be made up by the students with the help of the creation literature now available.

Any well informed student, can out perform any evolution teacher in the creation-evolution controversy, because truth is on his side. Most biology teachers, while they teach the evolution concepts in the book, have very little specific knowledge of the controversy. The intent is not to embarrass the teacher but to inform both the teacher and the other students.

In 1997, I challenged a textbook in a major high school in Fairfax County, Virginia concerning the derogation of the Christian religion in their biology text book. It was the Thomas Jefferson High School for Science and Technology "TJ" for short. The school was recently featured in the Dec. 10, 2007 issue of U.S. News and World Report, as the best high school in America. Mr. Geoffrey Jones was the principal at the time and was very helpful. He called a meeting of all the biology teachers and we discussed the matter for one hour. At the end of the meeting the only comment, by the teachers, was they didn't teach evolution as a fact, but as a theory. The lack of interest and any detailed knowledge of the subject by most teachers, was obvious.

All Christians should be well familiar with creation organizations such as Answers in Genesis and The Institute for Creation Research, as well as others. There is now an enormous amount of literature available that will strengthen anyone's belief in creation. Answers in Genesis recently completed a beautiful, multi-million dollar creation museum, near Cincinnati that is a tremendous asset to the real Biblical account of creation. Both groups publish books and also magazines that are invaluable to any Christian. These and other Christian and creation organizations can be contacted through the internet. Support placing creation literature in your church library.

With a renewed awakening of our Christian citizens, a lot of hard work, and with God's blessing we may yet turn this nation back to its basic moral foundation.

BIBLIOGRAPHY

Below is a listing of books and references I have obtained or reviewed through the years. These have contributed to the basic background and understanding that I attribute to my interest in writing this book. The list includes books by pastors, creationists, Atheists, Christians, theistic evolutionists, attorneys and others. To be knowledgeable in any controversy, one must understand both the arguments for and against what he believes. In addition to the books listed, I also have attended numerous lectures and debates, and obtained and viewed dozens of video tapes, as well as collecting well over a hundred magazines, over the past twenty years or so.

Darwin's Black Box .... Michael Behe

Acts and Facts .... Assorted issues
                                    Institute for Creation Research

Biological Science, A Molecular Approach .... BSCS Blue Version 7th Ed.

The Origin of Species .... Charles Darwin

Evolution and the Myth of Creationism .... Tim M. Berra

Defeating Darwinism by Opening Minds ... Phillip E. Johnson

History's Wildest Guess .... Dale Crowley Jr.

The Origin of Species Revisited, Vol.1 & 11 .... W. R. Bird

Encyclopedia Americana 1952

What is Creation Science .... Henry M. Morris & Gary E. Parker

The Collapse of Evolution .... Scott M. Huse

Science and Creationism .... edited by Ashley Montagn

Creation and the Modern Christian .... Henry M. Morris

Evolution: Fact, Fraud or Faith .... Don Boys

Origins and Destiny .... Dr. Robert Gangle

Of Pandas and People .... Davis & Kenyon

Process and Pattern in Evolution .... Charlotte J. Ayers

Evolution: Bone of Contention .... Sylvia Baker

Science and Creationism .... A View from the
National Academy of Sciences

In the Beginning .... Walt Brown

The Young Earth .... John D. Morris

From Darkness to Light:
Monarch the Miracle Butterfly .... John H. Poivier

The Decade of Creation .... Henry Morris, Donald Rohver

The Evidence for Creation .... McLean-Oakland-McLean

The Troubled Waters of Evolution .... Henry Morris

Creation: The Facts of Life .... Gary Parker

Science Scripture and the Young Earth .... Henry Morris &
John Morris

The World that Perished .... John C. Whitcomb

The Fingerprint of God .... Hugh Ross

Teaching Creation Science in Public Schools ...... Duane Gish

The Lie: Evolution .... Ken Ham

Evolution, Challenge of the Fossil Record .... Duane T. Gish

The Genesis Flood .... Johnn C. Whitcomb & Henry Morris ....

The Ordeal of Edward Bushell .... Godfrey D Lehman

The Genesis Solution .... Ken Ham & Paul Taylor

Darwin on Trial Philip E. Johnson

Reason in the Balance .... Philip E. Johnson

Living: An Introduction to Biology .... Stanley & Andrykovich

The Decade of Creation .... Henry Morris, Donald Rohver

The Natural Limits to Biological Change .... Lane Lester & Raymond Bohlin

Creation ex Nihilo .... Magazines(dozens)

In The Beginning:
God And the Six Day Creation .... William Nowers

The God Delusion .... Richard Dawkins

When Nations Die .... Jim Nelson Black

Abandonment Theology .... John W. Chalfant

Finding Darwin's God .... Kenneth R. Miller

The Federalist Papers .... Hamilton-Madison- Jay

Nine Men against America .... Rosalie M. Gordon

Original Intent .... David Barton

*God's Signature over the
Nation's Capital* .... Catherine Millard

*The American Covenant:
The Untold Story* .... Foster & Swanson

Godless, The Church of Liberalism .... Ann Coulter

Power to the People .... Laura Ingraham

The Bible .... King James Version

Wall of Misconception .... Peter A. Lillback

Blacklisted by History .... M. Stanton Evans

Evolution Exposed .... Roger Patterson